AGENT of DEATH

The Memoirs of an Executioner

ROBERT GREENE ELLIOTT

CONTENTS

"THAT'S A JOB I'D LIKE"

It was my parents' fondest wish that I become a Methodist minister. Weeks before I was born, Father said to Mother: "Martha, I hope it's a boy. If it is, let's name him after Reverend Greene. I'd like the lad to follow in the good man's footsteps."

Mother nodded approvingly, her heart warming at the thought that a son of hers might some day be a clergyman. She prayed long and often that this would be so.

Only part of my parents' hopes for me was realized. Shortly after my birth, I was christened Robert Greene Elliott, as Father had wanted. But I never gave any thought to studying for the ministry. Fate had other plans for me.

Neither Father nor Mother lived to see the day when I was to act as an agent of death. The former died when I was seven; the latter, in 1902—a year and a half before I performed my first execution at the order of the State of New York. However, had they lived until then, I believe they would have understood, just as have my wife and children.

Since assuming the role of official executioner for six Eastern states, I have thrown the switch which has hurled into eternity three hundred and eighty-seven occupants of the electric chair. This is the largest number of human

1

beings that any executioner has put to death by the lethal current.

These people, who it was decided had forfeited the right to live, have represented all strata of society. Some have come from the slums; others, from the mansions of the rich. Five of them have been woman. Most have been unknown, except for the brief notice which their trials and subsequent executions brought them. The names of a few, such as Bruno Richard Hauptmann, Nicola Sacco, Bartolomeo Vanzetti, Ruth Snyder, and Henry Judd Gray, have been on the lips of millions.

I have not found it easy to watch these wretch creatures die, convicted murderers though they were. Nor have I without some difficulty closed the electric switch to send them to meet their God.

But I must add—and I hope it will not be interpreted as the reaction of a calloused heart and mind—that have never permitted my work to trouble me. The decision that a man must pay with his life for the crime he committed has been made long before his appoint hour with death. It has been made by the commonwealth which has chosen me to carry out the sentence of the court. My job is to see that this is done as humanely as possible. Outside of that, my responsibility for this individual's untimely death is no greater than that of any other member of a society which endorses or condones capital punishment.

This comment is not for the purpose of justifying my duties as executioner—for, frankly speaking, I believe no justification by me is necessary. My object in mentioning it is that there can be a clearer understanding of how I view the grim business in which I have been engaged for so many years.

From the time it became known that I was an execut-ioner, I have had numerous opportunities to capitalize my unusual position. Offers which would have meant thousands of dollars to me have preceded or immediately followed most of the sensational cases. These have declined without a moment's hesitation.

While my name has appeared in hundreds of printed stories about executions, I have never sought publicity. If anything, I have gone out of my way to avoid it. Several years ago, an association of newspaper photographers in convention voted me the most difficult man in America to photograph. Perhaps the fact that I have shunned notoriety is one of the reasons I have received so much of it.

Unfortunately, a great deal has been written and said about me that is untrue. I have been, intention or otherwise, painted as some kind of ogre. Even pictures of me have been retouched so I would resemble something akin to the loathsome Mr. Hyde. After reading many of the distorted descriptions of my work, I can readily understand the popular impression that people run for cover when I walk down the street; that I live a very unnatural life, and that my family and I are lonely and friendless.

Were it not for these falsehoods and the fact that I have several grandchildren who will some day hear these ridiculous tales, I would never have consented to record in permanent form this account of my life and experiences. If my story has any public value or interest, then I, and not somebody else, should be the one to tell it.

My father, Thomas Elliott, came to America from County Cavan, Ireland, at the age of thirty, and purchased a large fruit farm in Monroe County, New York. There he met and married my mother, Martha Rowley.

I was born in Hamlin, New York, on January 27, 1874, the fifth of six children. The first child, a girl named Eva, was fatally scalded at the age of three when a pail of hot water accidentally fell on her. The second was a boy, but he lived only an hour. Another sister, also named Eva (now a resident of Detroit), was the third. She was followed by Emma, who died shortly after her twenty-fourth birthday. A boy, Thomas, came after me; but he died at the end of a year.

There was nothing in my happy boyhood to forecast the unusual or the grim. My life differed little from that of

3

any other normal farm boy. I loved to roam fields and the woods, and never passed up an opportunity to accompany my father on a visit to the orchard. Besides many peach and pear trees, more than a thousand apple trees were on the place—a fact about which I freely boasted to my playmates.

Our farm joined the Rome, Watertown and Ogdensburg Railroad, and the infrequent trains which passed over this line always thrilled me. One night at the dinner table, I declared with childlike certainty that I was going to be a railroad engineer some day. The announcement was met by a long silence, finally broken by my father.

"That's a long way off, son, and you'll probably change our mind by then. Mother and I hope you'll be a preacher. A preacher, you know, does a lot of good in this world, and that's what we'd like you to do."

This was the first and last time that either of my parents spoke to me of their ambitions for my future. However, my sister, Eva, has told me that they confided their dreams to others on numerous occasions.

It has always seemed odd to me that the thought of studying for the ministry never entered my mind, for as a boy I was always surrounded by religious influences. Father and Mother were very pious. All of us regularly attended church and Sunday school a mile half down the road, unless prevented by deep snows, heavy rains, or sickness. Grace was said at every meal, and Father or Mother read the Bible and offered a prayer before we went to bed.

An incident occurred in my boyhood which I shall regret. My father was mild-mannered and did not often lose his temper. One evening while I was watching a farmhand milk a cow, the animal kicked over the pail. Angered at what had happened, the helper cursed the cow. My father, who was only a short distance away, heard the profanity. He dropped what he was doing, walked over to the man, and shook him violently.

4

"Don't you ever let me hear you swear in front of a child again!" Father ordered.

The somewhat bewildered young man meekly answered, "No, sir."

On our way to the house, Father put his hand on my shoulder. "Bob," he said, "it's wrong to curse. You must never, never take the Lord's name in vain."

Father's counsel has remained with me throughout my life. Although I have many faults, profanity is not one of them.

My schooling began when I was five–but almost started a year earlier. A few days after my fourth birthday, Father took me to the little one-room schoolhouse not far from the farm. While waiting for the teacher to give me attention, I did something (I cannot recall just what) that caused the class to laugh. The teacher asked my age, and when I informed her, promptly sent me home with instructions not to return until I was five. I have always suspected that she thought me mischievous, and wanted another year before being compelled to add my name to the roll.

In those days, schoolteachers in our section were poorly paid. As part of their compensation, they lived at the various homes in the district, changing their residence periodically. I was extremely happy when it was my parents' turn to play host to the teacher, who seemed quite willing to answer questions for which there was no time during school hours.

Father died in the summer of 1881 after a few months' illness. Although I was only a small boy, I missed him a great deal. Mother remained on the farm, but a year later found the management of the property too much for her. My sister, Eva, had married and left for the West, and debts were beginning to pile up.

When Mother decided to break up housekeeping, I was sent to live with a James Stewart, whose farm was about two miles from our place. He had a son, Robert, who was just my age, and the two of us got along very well. Meanwhile, my mother went with a sister-in-law. A cousin, Mrs. Cora Robinson, of Brockport, New York took me a year later. Until I was ten, I divided my time between Cousin Cora and Aunt Phoebe Rowley.

On the day before Christmas in 1884, I was welcomed to the farm of Cousin Lydia and her husband, Nelson Garlock, in Sheridan, New York, where I stayed until I was sixteen. The Garlocks were good people, and gave me a wonderful home. There I arose every morning at five o'clock, worked until time for school, and did chores when I returned late in the afternoon.

It was while living in Sheridan that I first became interested in electricity—a force that I, at the state's command, was to employ later in life to send condemned prisoners to their doom. Working for the Garlocks was an old farmhand by the name of Herbert Terrell, who had been a telegraph operator. He told me about electricity and its wonders.

"Electricity is going to be the most remarkable power man ever worked with," he said enthusiastically. "The fact that we can send messages with it and use it for light is marvelous enough. But these things are only the beginning."

I was in his company every possible minute, and we became close friends. At times, I begged to stay home from school to talk with him, but was not permitted to do this. So fascinated was I with Terrell's explanation of the telegraph and its importance to the world that I forgot about my childish ambition to become a railroad engineer. A telegraph operator was now more to my liking.

When not spending my spare time with the old farmhand, I was reading everything I could lay hands on which had something to do with the subject of electricity. I acquired two books on light and heat, and these I read and reread. The daily newspaper delivered to the Garlocks published a column on science, which I followed religiously.

The bill substituting electrocution for hanging in New York State was signed by Governor David B. Hill on June 4, 1888. Although only fourteen at the time, I distinctly

6

remember hearing discussed the change in the method of executing murderers. Terrell was especially interested, for he wondered how the new law was to be put into effect.

Legal death by electricity had been the subject of considerable debate for several years. In his annual message to the New York Legislature in 1885, Governor Hill had recommended:

The present mode of executing criminals by hanging has come down to us from the Dark Ages, and it may well be questioned whether the science of the present day cannot provide a means for taking the lives of such as are condemned to die in a less barbarous manner. I commend this suggestion to the consideration of the Legislature.

A commission was appointed in 1886 to investigate and report the most humane and practical method of carrying out the sentence of death for capital offenses. After exhaustive study, this group of scientists proposed electrocution, and the change resulted. Thus came into being those grim words: "The sentence of the court is that a current of electricity be passed through your body until you are dead—and may God have mercy on your soul."

Under the new law, applicable to all murders committed in the state after January 1, 1889, the judge imposing the sentence was merely to set the week within which the condemned was to be executed. The exact day and hour were left to the warden's discretion. Following sentence, the doomed prisoner was to be taken immediately by the sheriff of the county to one of the three state prisons where executions were to be performed. There he was to be kept in solitary confinement until the day of his death—to be visited only by officers or by his relatives, physician, clergyman, or counsel.

To prevent future executions from becoming Roman holidays for the morbidly curious, the statute limited those to be present to prison authorities, clergymen, doctors, and official witnesses. After the condemned was put to death and an autopsy performed, relatives could claim the body. Otherwise, it was to be buried within the prison grounds.

The public, influenced by scathing newspaper editorials and blasts from pulpit and platform, vigorously protested the adoption of electrocution. There were those who expressed serious doubt that this invisible force would kill. Others who admitted its death-dealing potentialities wondered whether electricity was more humane than the rope, or saw no reason to improve on the method of legal killing. As I heard one farmer express it, "Hanging's good enough for any murderer."

In the midst of this furor, the state set about to devise a means of carrying out the new law. After weird experiments on various animals, the electric chair was decided upon. State Superintendent of Prisons Austin Lathrope delegated the job of building such a device to Edwin F. Davis, an electrician who was later to playa an important part in my life. Construction of the chair got under way at once in Auburn Prison's woodworking shop, and for a while proceeded with the utmost secrecy.

As the chair neared completion, details of it leaked out. Newspapers and magazines devoted considerable space to pictorial and word descriptions of the devastating piece of furniture. Accounts of the difficulties which the prison authorities were having with manufacturers of electrical equipment were widely circulated. Despite all this, I paid little attention to the subject–either because I was too young or at the time regarded electricity in a purely constructive, and not destructive, sense.

After many changes, the death chair was finally ready for its premiere. I read in a newspaper how the finished product looked. The instrument, square and made of oak, was secured to the floor. The high back sloped slightly, and the arms were broad. It was not at all uncomfortable.

Three wooden braces were across the back. Fastened two was a cushion of hard rubber, against condemned's head and back rested. A figure-4 framework (no longer in use) ran up from the top of the chair, and was adjustable to conform to the height of the prisoner.

Through the point of this passed a wire leading to the head electrode. The body electrode was attached to the base of the chair.

Bell-shaped, the electrodes by which the current entered and left the body were four inches in diameter. They consisted of a rubber cup enclosing a metal disk faced with a layer of sponge.

Large, strong leather straps were employed to hold the person in the chair while the current was coursing through his body. Originally, there was a footrest; but this was discarded several months before the completion of the work.

Then came the first electrocution—and my first real interest in the electric chair. In Buffalo, on March 29, 1889, William Kemmler killed his mistress, Tillie Zeigler, with a hatchet. He was speedily convicted and sentenced to die. However, it was not until August 6, 1890, that he finally paid his debt to society. At that time, I was working for a farmer named Rush Minor, in Sheridan, New York, and gathered information as to what happened at Kemmler's execution from newspaper accounts, from a young man visiting in the town, and later from Davis himself.

A great array of physicians had gone to Auburn for the execution. Among those who were to act as witnesses was Dr. A. P. Southwick, of Buffalo, father of the electrocution law. Kemmler, who apparently had been apprised of the march of events, realized that he was dying not alone for the crime he had committed, but for science as well.

Although, Kemmler's departure from this world had been set for the week of August 3, Warden Charles F. Durston kept the fatal day a secret. At 5:30 o'clock on the morning of the sixth, the warden had the proprietor of the hotel at which the witnesses were staying rouse them from their beds and tell them to report at the prison.

After all had assembled in the death chamber and were seated in a semicircle around the electric chair which had been built the previous year, Warden Durston went for Kemmler. Dressed better than he had ever been before, the condemned man walked into the room with a light, quick step. It was obvious that he knew he was the center of attraction, and enjoyed the interest he was creating.

The warden, for some reason, offered Kemmler a chair, and the short, black-bearded man sat down on it directly in front of the death seat. Then, like a master of ceremonies announcing an act, Durston said, "Gentlemen, this is William Kemmler."

The murderer nodded slightly in acknowledgment, and remarked: "The newspapers have been saying a lot of things about me which were not so. I wish you all good luck in this world. I believe I am going to a good place."

His speech ended, Kemmler arose.

"Now we'll get ready, William," declared the warden. "Let me take off your coat."

The man over whom death was hovering refused all assistance, and tossed his coat over the back of the chair from which he had just risen. He was about to remove his waistcoat when the warden told him this would be unnecessary, as it had been slit up the back. Kemmler's shirt was then cut away, baring the flesh where the lower electrode was to be applied.

Earlier in the morning, Kemmler had pleaded with Deputy Sheriff Veiling: "Joe, I want you to stick by me through this thing. Don't let them experiment on me more than they ought to."

Veiling now set the murderer in the chair, and began to strap him in. His hands shook, causing him to fumble with the straps.

"Don't get excited, Joe," said Kemmler. "I want you to make a good job of this."

When the head electrode was put in position by the warden, Kemmler moved his head from side to side to indicate that it was not snug. "I guess you'd better make that a little tighter, Mr. Durston," he suggested.

This was done, and the lower electrode was applied at the base of the back, rather than on the leg as it is today.

"Good-by, William," called the warden after the mask had been placed over the condemned man's face.

"Good-by," feebly came the voice from the chair.

Warden Durston knocked twice on the door of the room adjoining the death chamber. The executioner, hidden from view, threw the switch, sending 1,000 volts ripping through Kemmler's body. After seventeen seconds—about one-eighth as long as I keep the current for an electrocution—the doctors ordered the power shut off. They then gathered around the figure in the chair. A New York *World* reporter related what happened next:

Suddenly the breast heaved. There was a straining at the straps which bound him.... The man was alive. Warden, physicians, everybody, lost their wits. There was a startled cry for the current to be turned on again. Signals, only half understood, were given to those in the next room at the switchboard. When they knew what had happened, they were prompt to act, and the switch-handle could be heard it was pulled back and forth, breaking the deadly current into jets.

Electricity flowed through the body for four minutes the second time. Thus was the first man electrocuted by the state—deliberately and legally, but not very efficiently.

There followed a loud outcry of "unnecessary brutality from the public and the press. Some newspapers described the execution as a horror. Even the doctors disagreed on its success. However, Dr. Southwick, who, as I mentioned before, had had the law introduced into the legislature, expressed satisfaction.

Declaring that the result of Kemmler's execution "strongly condemns this method of putting criminals—as very cruel and very shocking," *The World* urged immediate repeal of the law. "So long as it stands, convictions for capital offenses will be difficult to the point of impossibility," the editorial insisted. "Juries will not willingly condemn men to death by torture. So long as capital punishment is maintained, old-fashioned hanging is good enough, provided it is administered by trained and skillful hangmen."

The New York Times was among the large and influential papers that did not share this opinion. "It would be absurd to talk of abandoning the law and going back to the barbarism of hanging," commented this publication, "and it would be as puerile to propose to abolish capital punishment because the new mode of execution was botched in its first application."

Public resentment finally subsided, and death by electricity continued in New York as the penalty for first-degree murder. With the improvement in equipment and efficiency, the electric chair was adopted by many other states. Consequently, Kemmler became the pioneer of the long and lengthening line of the condemned who have followed him to death by electric shock.

Both before and after the first electrocution, there was considerable speculation as to who was designated to throw the fatal switch. At first, it was rumored that the job would fall to Charles R. Barnes, of Rochester, New York, who was to be in the dynamo room several hundred feet from the death chamber. He quickly denied this.

"I see it is said in the morning papers in a dispatch from Auburn that I am to close the switch which sends the current to the chair in which Kemmler is to be executed," Barnes told reporters. "That is not so. My duty is to regulate the current at one switch. Another person will close a second switch and will send the current, which I have regulated, to the chair."

As Electrician Davis had supervised the construction of the chair and was in charge of the switchboard when Kemmler died, many were convinced that he was the executioner.

Years later, after he had become official executioner, Davis to me about the Kemmler case. While he was unwilling to acknowledge that the execution was a bungled job, he did admit that the apparatus was not all it should have been. For one thing, he said, the electrodes were too small, and caused too much burning of the body.

This situation was corrected shortly afterward–the surface area of the electrodes was increased, and the amount of regulated voltage was stepped up. Also, the design of the chair was revised.

From the information Davis gave me, I believe Kemmler died without pain. I feel convinced that the first shock rendered him unconscious–just as it does now to the person strapped in the chair. However, it is understandable why the witnesses came away with the impression that the man had suffered.

The Kemmler execution was not the only one which caused criticism of the electrocution law and of those who carried it out. There were several other misadventures. For instance, on July 27, 1893, a man was put to death at Auburn Prison in a manner that created more than a mild sensation.

A convict, William G. Taylor, had cold-bloodedly murdered a fellow prisoner, and the state demanded his life in payment. At the moment that the first electric shock struck him, his legs stiffened, tearing away the front part of the chair to which his ankles were strapped. The current was turned off, a guard obtained a box and placed it under the chair, and the execution continued.

But there was more trouble ahead. As the doctors examined the body after the last shock, they found that the man was still breathing. The warden promptly ordered another application of the current; but when Davis threw the switch, none came. The executioner hastened to the powerhouse, returning in a few minutes with the information that the generator had burned out. This was an emergency for which no one, not even Davis, could have been prepared.

Taylor was taken from the chair and placed on a cot which had been brought into the death chamber. Drugs were administered to prevent pain in the remote event that he should regain consciousness. Meanwhile, electricians and other citizens were stringing wires over the prison walls from the city's power plant. An hour passed before all was ready.

Although the murderer had died while the work was going on, his limp form was placed in the chair, and current flowed through it for half a minute. The prison authorities then decided that justice had been done as prescribed by law.

Davis and I talked about this harrowing experience some years later. He explained that the machinery broke down because the generator was taxed beyond capacity at executions, more current being required on these occasions. He particularly regretted the opportunity the incident afforded opponents of electrocution to renew their clamoring for abolition of the electric chair, which he regarded as more humane than the rope.

Excitement usually attended all of the early executions. Crowds of morbidly curious people swarmed outside the prison. Newspapermen, pressed by their editors every possible detail, went so far as to erect scaffolds from which they could look into the prison yard and try to obtain information through the movements of officers inside.

By the time I reached sixteen, electric power and its limitless possibilities so fascinated me that I decided definitely to become an electrical engineer. No one objected, not even Mother; but I did learn years later that she found it difficult to mask her disappointment. From me, however, she always managed to hide her feelings

Having determined on a career, I now wanted to pursue seriously the study of electricity. The Brockport Normal School was the only educational institution the vicinity where I could learn about the subject. This, of course, was for the training of teachers, and, unfortunately, was not interested in a young man with other ambitions.

Ostensibly as a prospective teacher, I finally entered the school, and spent a little more than two years there. I majored in mathematics and physics. Long before I had advanced to the latter subject, I would sneak into the class if I had a free period. The physics professor observed this, and asked me one day to remain after the other students had gone.

"Young man," he said sternly, "I see you in my class on frequent occasions, yet your name is not on my roll. You have no right here, and I should make you leave or report you." Then more sympathetically: "But I'm not going to. I used to do the same thing myself, so it would hardly be fair for me to keep you out. Come as often as you like."

I joined the class shortly after that, and became absorbed in physics as it related to electricity far more than was necessary for one actually training to be an instructor. Although he never spoke to me about it, I am sure the professor suspected that I never intended to teach.

While attending normal school, I stayed part of the time with Aunt Phoebe, and the rest with George Allen, a manufacturer of harvesting machinery for whom I worked for my board. The Allens lived only a short distance from the Brockport electric light plant, where I spent all my spare time. Realizing that I was anxious to learn, Alex McMullen, the chief engineer, explained how the machinery operated, and willingly answered my many questions.

The engineer took me aside one day and confided that an extra man would be needed shortly at the plant. At the proper time, I applied for the post—and got it. Then I quit school. Much to my surprise and delight, McMullen permitted me to start the 125-horsepower Cooper Corliss engine the first night I went to work. Like any eighteen-year-old boy on his first job, I was as proud as a peacock.

Prior to my employment at the power plant, I had paid scant attention to newspaper accounts of murders and the trials which followed. Now, with time on my hands during the night, I found myself reading them. The first murder case in which I became intensely interested was that of Lizzie Borden. Lizzie was alleged to have killed her father and stepmother in Massachusetts, and was tried for the crime. Columns were devoted to her sensational trial at New Bedford, and not a single detail escaped my eye.

Although the newspaper stories convicted her in my mind, I was glad to earn of her acquittal on that June day in 1893.

A crime occurred nine months later that was to result in the first inexplicable incident of my life. On March 6, 1894, in an election dispute at Troy, New York, a watcher at the polls was killed, and another shot, but not fatally. Bartholomew Shea was arrested for the murder; John B. McGough was charged with the other shooting. At their trials, the former was convicted of first-degree murder, and sentenced to die. The latter, also, was found guilty, receiving a long prison term.

I was talking with George Tozier, son of a Brockport druggist, when the papers reached us with the news that Shea was to be electrocuted. Strangely enough, my thoughts turned from the doomed man to the one who, by the mere closing of an electric switch, would quickly dispatch Shea into the next world.

"Think of the executioner's great responsibility," I declared. "That's a job I'd like to have."

An expression of horror spread over Tozier's face. He looked at me unbelievingly, as though he had not heard correctly. Then the full significance of what I had said dawned on me. I hurriedly changed the subject, and I guess he did not take my statement seriously. Surely neither of us ever dreamed that the day would come when I was to be engaged in such work.

What impelled that remark, I do not know. Often I have tried to explain it to myself, but without success. Perhaps I entertained the opinion that a high degree of science was required to kill human beings painlessly; that the man who served as executioner must be a clever electrician.

An appeal and two reprieves delayed Shea's execution. I was at Avon, New York, at the time, having gone there in the summer of 1895 to start the operation of the town's lighting plant, which had been partly installed. The second reprieve came after McGough confessed" to the warden of Clinton Prison that he, and not Shea, had fired the fatal shot. But several weeks' investigation failed to convince the authorities, and Governor Morton refused to intervene further. Shea went to his death on February 11, 1896, protesting his innocence to the very end.

Immediately after the execution, McGough was permitted to talk to newspaper reporters. He was quoted as having said:

"Before God, I tell you Shea was innocent. I killed Ross. Shea died for something he never did. They murdered him. Why, those witnesses swore as they were told. If Shea had not been picked out as the man, I would have been, and all the witnesses who swore to Shea's having shot Ross would have sworn with the same positiveness that I did. I am not afraid of the consequences. My conscience bothers me more than anything else. Don't you suppose I'll always think of that poor fellow dying today for something I did? I don't care what they do with me."

Incidentally, I met McGough at Clinton Prison some years later while I was chief engineer there. He worked for me a short time, and we talked of many things. But no mention was ever made of Shea's execution.

One night McGough and I were walking from the powerhouse to the building in which his cell was located. It was a beautiful, clear night, and I remarked about it.

"Yes, it is beautiful," he said, glancing skyward "Look at those stars up there. This is the first time I've seen them overhead in eighteen long years."

I considered his statement rather peculiar until the next day. Then I learned from the principal keeper that up to that time, McGough had never been allowed outside his cell after dark.

At Avon, with the help of Arthur Neafie, another electrician, I operated the small community's light plant. We wired stores and residences, and the number of places using electricity grew surprisingly. The engines were started up late in the afternoon when was dark enough to require light, and kept going until midnight. Sometimes they were operated in the morning during the winter months.

In our spare time, Neafie and I went bicycle riding. On one of these occasions, I met a laughing, bright eyed schoolteacher—Addie Belle Hocmer. It must hat been a case of love at first sight, for, from that time, showered all my attentions only on her. When she went to Argyle, New York, to teach, I became dissatisfied, Avon and wanted to be near her.

Announcement was made about that time of an examination for assistant electrician at Clinton Prison in Dannemora. The plant was being operated by convicts; but after one of them escaped, it was decided to place men from the outside in charge of the powerhouse. This seemed like the opportunity for which I had been waiting, so I took the test. When the names eligible candidates were made public, I headed the list. Within a few days, word came that I was to report at the penitentiary.

Leaving my mother, sister, and niece Avon (where they had been living with me), I assumed my duties at the prison on March 1, 1898. Maxwell Cooley had been appointed chief electrician there, and the two of us resided within the prison walls.

Anxious for advancement, I took the examination for electrical engineer about six months later. Again I stood at the top of the list. When Cooley obtained a position in Washington, D. C., that December, Warden Walter N. Thayer named me to the vacated post.

All during this time, I was seeing my schoolteacher-sweetheart as frequently as possible. At each meeting, I tried to persuade her that life in the prison town was preferable to instructing Argyle's young hopefuls. I must have convinced her, for we were married in June, 1899. My mother and my niece, who had moved to Dannemora that spring, came to live with us.

I have often wondered whether my wife would have accepted me could she have foreseen the strange twist of fate that some day was to make me an executioner. But of one thing I am certain: without her, my unusual life could not have been as nearly normal as it has been.

ONE WHO SURVIVED BRIEFLY

My first acquaintance with legal killing by manmade lightning came at Dannemora. The prison plant furnished current for the electric chair. As chief electrician, I was in charge of the powerhouse, and it was my job to operate the machinery for executions.

Although I should have known, it never occurred to me when I accepted the post that this was to be part of my work. In fact, nearly four years passed before I was called upon to supply the current which was to snuff out a man's life.

I had been in the death chamber and had seen the chair many times prior to my having anything to do with an execution. I often went to the cheerless room to do electrical repair work or to take curious visitors through the place.

In those days, the public was permitted to inspect the prisons. I was occasionally asked by the warden or the principal keeper to conduct people around the premises, showing them the cells, shops, and other things of interest. The electric chair seemed to hold a horrible fascination for everybody, including women; and all invariably wanted to be shown the death chamber. Once inside, most of them were not satisfied until they had sat in the forbidding instrument which the state had made a symbol of justice.

The first time that I sat in the chair was at the request of the wife of a prominent state official. I was escorting her and several other women on a tour of the prison, and we came to the execution chamber. As all were afraid to sit in the chair themselves, they asked me to oblige.

"I've always wanted to see how a man would look in the electric chair," said the official's wife. "Would you mind sitting down and being strapped in?"

I had no objection, and got a guard to help me. He strapped me in just as he would have done a person doomed to die. Then he stepped aside so the women could witness the result of his handiwork.

While they were watching me, I tried to move; but the broad leather straps held me fast. Although I knew there was no danger—the electrodes had not been applied to my body and no current could possibly reach the chair—a strange sensation engulfed me. I felt so completely helpless. I realized that, no matter how hard I might struggle, I could not free myself. I wondered whether those who had been put to death in this fashion had felt the same way, only, of course, to a far greater degree.

It was with a certain sense of relief that I got up from the chair after the straps had been unbuckled. Since that day, I have sat and been strapped in an electric chair numerous times in order that it could be properly adjusted to accommodate the poor creature about to be executed. Even the black mask has been placed over my face, and electrodes have been fastened to my head and leg. But I have never again experienced the same emotions.

On June 22, 1901, a George Middleton, of Pottersville, New York, killed his wife in a fit of jealousy. He was convicted, and sent to Clinton Prison for execution. July 29, 1902, was finally set as the date on which he must pay the supreme penalty. It was also the first time that I was required to furnish the power by which a human life would be stilled.

Davis, then the executioner, arrived at the penitentiary the previous afternoon. Warden George Deyo brought him down to the plant where I was working and introduced us. I observed that the man who threw the switch was small and wiry. He had piercing eyes, high cheekbones, and a drooping black mustache. I must admit that I was a bit uncomfortable in his presence–perhaps like others might be when meeting me for the first time. Davis apparently realized this, for he tried to put me at ease by engaging in conversation. He inquired about the plant, conditions at the prison, and my family (by this time I had a son, Robert, and a daughter, Frances). He told me about his hobby-bees–and how much enjoyment he got out of it.

"You know," he laughed, "bees might sting you; but it's a whole lot better than being 'stung' by a two-legged critter."

I agreed–and the ice was broken. We then got down to the grim business ahead of us, and Davis explained in detail exactly what I was to do the next day. All executions at Dannemora, unless delayed for some purpose, took place on Tuesday morning. For a number of years, the hour was 11:40 o'clock, because the prison needed the least power then. In 1904, the time was changed, for a reason that I will explain later.

As the electric plant was located in a building about seven hundred feet from the death chamber, communication was by a system of bells. There were five of these signals. The first, which was to be given fifteen or twenty minutes before the condemned began to walk "the last mile," meant that I should start the engine. At the second bell, I was to throw the switch which sent the current over the wires to the execution chamber. More current was to be turned on at the third signal; but this was really unnecessary, for all that the generator would produce was dispatched originally. The fourth bell was to inform me to lower the amount of current, and at the fifth signal, I was to turn it off and stop the engine.

To be certain that I clearly understood what was expected of me, we planned to rehearse everything about ten o'clock the next morning when Davis was to test the apparatus in the death chamber. We then parted, the executioner going to a hotel until his services were needed and I home to dinner.

My wife was fully aware of the fact that, barring intervention by the governor, Middleton had only a few hours to live. She also knew of the role that I was to play in sending the man to his doom. Confident that my task was distasteful to her, I anticipated some comment. But there was none. Her silence made things much easier for me, and I was grateful.

Shortly before ten the following morning, I went up to the death chamber. Davis was busy attaching two sponges about the size of a man's hand to a large piece of beef. To each sponge he fastened one of the wires leading to the chair. Looking up from his work, he greeted me pleasantly, and explained that he employed the meat (sometimes weighing as much as fifteen pounds) to determine whether or not current was passing through the chair. Seven amperes ordinarily went through the meat, he said. I learned later that after the executioner had finished with the beef, an officer took it to the boiler house and tossed it into the furnace, much to the disappointment of convicts who worked around the death house and would have liked to eat it.

Down at the plant, I replaced the 1,000 volt armature on one of the prison's two generators with a 1,700 volt armature. Then I waited for the signal to start the engine. It finally came, and Davis and I went through the procedure we had agreed upon the afternoon before. After the final bell, Davis came down and told me that I had followed instructions perfectly. Now I was to wait until the state was ready to take up its option on Middleton's life.

As the minutes ticked by, I grew nervous, as did the convicts who helped me at the plant. All of these men were trusties, and several were lifers. None of us spoke of our task, although I am sure it was uppermost in our minds. During Middleton's stay in the death house, I had visited that part of the prison several times, but had never

22

laid eyes on the wife-slayer. I was glad I had not seen him.

I thought of Middleton's crime, of the untold suffering it had brought to others. I thought of the four small children who would be orphaned when the fifth bell sounded that day. I felt sorry for them, just as I have so many times pitied the families of those I have been ordered to execute.

The ringing of the bell aroused me from my thoughts. I ran over to the engine and started it. Fifteen minutes later came the second signal. Middleton was walking his "last mile." The bell rang again to increase the current. The engine began to labor; the ammeter registered ten amperes. I knew that electricity was passing through the doomed man's body.

At that moment, there flashed through my mind the remark I had made years earlier about wanting to be an executioner. Was I not almost one now? I asked myself. Did not the fact that I supplied the lethal current place me on a par with Davis? No, I was only an electrician in the employ of the state—a man whose job it was to operate a power plant.

It was customary in those days to administer more than one electric shock. The first was of two or three minutes' duration, after which the doctors listened with their stethoscopes to ascertain whether the heart was still beating. A second application of current followed immediately, lasting for about a minute. The doctors listened again, and usually pronounced the man dead. However, another half-minute shock was sent through the body to make certain that all life was extinct. Sometimes as many as six shocks were necessary to stop heart action. In Middleton's case, four were required.

After what seemed an eternity, the fourth bell sounded—and then the fifth. I shut down the engine, and mopped the perspiration from my brow. Everything had functioned satisfactorily at the plant, and I hoped there had been no trouble in the death chamber. After changing armatures, I went up to the death house, where Davis was packing his electrodes and the doctors were performing the autopsy. I asked Davis how things had gone.

"Everything was fine," he replied. "Nothing out of the ordinary happened. The poor fellow took it like a man, and didn't say a word. Now I've got to catch that train." Davis hurried out of the prison, and I did not see him again until his next trip to Dannemora.

The plant had operated perfectly that day, but the time did come when the generator failed me during an execution. On that particular occasion, the machinery ran smoothly until after the fourth bell—the signal to reduce the current. Then the governor spring broke, and the engine stopped. I was almost panicky, for I knew that repairs would take some time. A few seconds later the bell sounded to cut off the current. Davis told me afterward that the doctors had pronounced the man dead just before the accident happened. Consequently, when he saw that there was no current, he simply had the body removed from the chair without administering a final shock. I shudder to think of what would have happened had the spring broken a minute or two sooner.

Except for the year when I worked at another state institution, I supplied the current for Clinton Prison's electric chair until Sing Sing Prison at Ossining was designated to perform all of New York's executions. As did my wife, my mother knew that this was part of my duties. But she never said anything to me about it, and, so far as I know, never criticized me before others.

One thing which pleased Mother very much was the interest that I took in religious work during my early years in the prison service. My wife and I regularly attended the Methodist Episcopal Church in Dannemora, and it was not long before we were asked to take a more active part. I became superintendent of the Sunday school, an office I held for several years. As head of this department, I was in charge of the service, and announced the hymns, frequently offered the prayer, and occasionally explained the lesson. I was also a member of the official board, and was chosen later as treasurer of the church.

The fact that my duties at the prison included furnishing current for the electric chair made no difference to the church people. Perhaps they were inclined to be more broad-minded than others in this respect because most of the men in the congregation were employed at the penitentiary in one capacity or another.

My mother died unexpectedly on Election Day in 1902. In October, she had fallen and broken her hip. All of us thought she was recovering; but complications set in, and she passed away on November 4. This was a severe blow to me, and I was many months getting over it.

Prison breaks during my first few years at Dannemora were repeated occurrences. After a convict had escaped, the services of everybody in the prison employ were required until the man had been found and returned to his cell. At such times, I usually answered the telephone. Calls came in almost constantly from people for miles around who thought—and sometimes correctly so—that they knew the whereabouts of the man or men we sought. Every "lead" was investigated.

A prisoner by the name of Crossman and another convict staged the first escape after I went to Clinton Prison. One October day in 1898, the two men reached the top of the wall by climbing a rope, which they had obtained in a manner unknown to the authorities. Entering the booth on the wall, they overpowered the guard and took his rifle. The jump of twenty-two feet to the ground inj man, but Crossman gained the woods without difficulty. The break was witnessed by a lifer working in the prison hospital, who gave the alarm. The escaped convicts' freedom was short-lived, for the prisoners were caught almost immediately. As punishment, both were placed in solitary confinement.

But Crossman's desire for the free air outside the prison burned as intensely as ever. So, in the spring of 1902, he tried it again—this time alone. He managed to make a hole from his cell to the attic, and, at four o'clock

25

one morning when no guard was within sight, crawled through it. Tearing away a section of the sheet-iron roof, the prisoner let himself down onto the bath house roof and got away. His absence from prison was longer this time, but he was finally returned. Solitary was again meted out to him.

The authorities decided that something must be done to prevent his escaping a third time. They were especially worried when he was in the yard, there being only a wall between him and the outside world. Someone suggested the ball and chain. With this fastened to one of his ankles, it was argued, Crossman would not be likely to try any more dashes for freedom. The idea the heavy weight was attached to the convict's leg.

However, this lasted only a few days. Although Crossman himself never complained about it, a protest was registered with the warden by somebody else. It was the first and only time I ever saw a ball and chain on a prisoner.

While most of the escapes were made by trusties who simply walked away, there were several cleverly planned breaks, such as that by Peter James and three associates in the summer of 1903. The convicts dug a tunnel about twenty feet from the tin shop cellar to an old storm sewer, and crept through it. They were back in the prison in four days. One of the men was badly wounded in attempting to avoid capture.

Because Kemmler was the first person to die in the electric chair, it is generally thought that he was the first to be sentenced under the electrocution law. This, however, is not true. The first murderer condemned to the chair was Joseph Chappleau, who killed a neighbor for poisoning his cows. His sentence was later commuted to life imprisonment, and he was sent to Dannemora.

I came to know Chappleau well. An excellent penman, he was assigned to the state shop, where he was bookkeeper. I chatted with him on my visits to the shop, and found him very intelligent. He never spoke of his crime or of his good fortune in having his life spared.

But another prisoner who barely escaped the chair was different. This man, who today is free and leading an honest life, not only would talk of the murder he committed, but also would boast of how close he came to being executed. He was painfully thin, which made him the object of many quips. When asked how much he weighed, he would usually reply, "Two ounces less than a straw hat."

After a few years in prison, the convict, whom I will call Jim, was given a responsible job. He was permitted to go anywhere on the premises, and usually served meals to the condemned. One morning he brought me word that I was to go to the death chamber to repair a light socket. He accompanied me, and remained in the room until I had finished.

I happened to turn around to pick up a tool when I noticed that Jim was sitting in the electric chair. He was maneuvering himself into the most comfortable position, and seemed entirely oblivious of the fact that I was staring at him.

Finally, he looked up and saw that I was watching. But he did not appear the least bit embarrassed.

"Not a bad piece of furniture, not at all," Jim remarked. "It's a lot more comfortable than I thought. But I guess the poor guys who *have* to sit in it don't think so. I almost had to, and would have if it hadn't been for the governor. Boy, was I happy when I heard about the commute."

At every opportunity from that day on, Jim would sneak into the death house to look at the chair. I think he got a certain amount of pleasure out of seeing the apparatus which might have ended his life.

As I mentioned before, convicts worked for me at the plant. Among them were men convicted of serious crimes. Most were model prisoners, rarely causing me any trouble. In fact, I reported only three of them during my entire twenty years at Dannemora. Two engaged in a fist fight; the third refused to carry out orders. After being punished, they were sent back to the powerhouse, and

27

their behavior then was above reproach. So far as I know, they harbored no ill will toward me for turning them in. At least, they never displayed any, and one wrote me a most friendly letter after he was released from prison.

One of my assistants was a fellow by the name of Joseph Brennan, who, in my opinion, should rank among the world's cleverest pickpockets. Whenever my watch was missing, I knew exactly where to find it. Joe had picked it so he could keep in practice, but always gave it back.

He told me an interesting story of how he was taught the art. When Joe was but a boy, his father would put a coin in the pocket of a woman's skirt, and tie a bell to the garment. Then he would hang up the skirt, and order the lad to get the money. If he jingled the bell in removing the coin, Joe was whipped. He was compelled to repeat this performance until he became an expert pickpocket. For pursuing such a "career," he served prison terms in Massachusetts, Louisiana, and New York.

In the fall of 1903, something occurred that, without my realizing it, brought me a step closer to the grim profession of executioner. Davis had patented the electrodes used at executions, and these he carried with him from prison to prison. This was a source of un-easiness to state officials, who wondered what would happen in the event of Davis' death. Who would throw the switch after he was gone? As he owned patents to part of the electrical apparatus, could New York continue to electrocute its convicted murderers? These questions were being asked in official circles, and the answers given made the situation even more confusing.

There was but one thing to do: purchase the patents and have Davis instruct several people in how to perform an execution. Those who thought of this plan had considered everything—except Davis. His inventions were not for sale, he said, and he was not disposed to train anybody for his job.

For two years, the executioner turned a deaf ear to all offers and representations. At last, for the handsome sum of $10,000 he agreed to transfer his patents to the State of New York, and to show two electricians how to officiate at legal killings.

Davis' first assistant was Edwin C. Currier, chief engineer at the Massachusetts State Prison in Charlestown. Superintendent of Prisons Cornelius V. Collins decided that I was to be the other, and sent word to Warden Deyo to have me witness the next execution at Dannemora. That, of course, was impossible, as I was needed at the power plant on such occasions.

Before I acted as Davis' assistant, Dannemora wrote a weird chapter in the history of man's punishment of man. The incident provided a case of a doomed prisoner's surviving briefly the power of electricity to kill. It occurred at the triple execution of the Van Wormer brothers in the fall of 1903.

Willis, Burton, and Fred Van Wormer were convicted of the brutal murder of their uncle, Peter A. Hallenbeck. Hallenbeck had foreclosed a mortgage on the property of the brothers' stepmother in Greendale, compelling them to move to Kinderhook. This caused bitterness, and the young men swore vengeance on their uncle.

On Christmas Eve, 1901, the three Van Wormers, with their cousin, Harvey Bruce, drove fourteen miles in a hired wagon to Hallenbeck's home. A short distance from the place, they turned their coats inside out and donned masks. Thus disguised, they proceeded to the house, where Hallenbeck, his wife, and aged mother were sitting in the living room.

A loud knock brought Hallenbeck to the kitchen door. Led by Burton, the four youths, armed with revolvers, backed him into the room. As the old man made a move to grapple with one of the group, he was riddled with bullets. Mrs. Hallenbeck ran into the kitchen when she heard the shots, and the masked intruders fired at her. Fortunately, she was not hit.

Betrayed by their footprints in the snow around the house, the four boys, who already had bad reputations in the community, were soon arrested. Bruce turned state's

29

evidence, and it was largely on his testimony that the brothers were convicted. He was sent to prison for eighteen years.

Then followed a long legal battle which was to keep the Van Wormers alive, and hopeful of escape from death in the chair, until October 1, 1903. I talked with them several times during their many months in the death house. They were always cheerful and certain that they would not be punished for their crime. To me, they seemed like fine young men—an opinion unsupported by their past record and by those who knew them intimately.

"They won't do anything to us," Burton said confidently. "We're just up here for a nice vacation. We'll be out in no time."

Although I did not share his optimism, I saw no reason to disillusion him.

Rumor spread throughout the prison on the day before they were to die that, for some reason, Davis would be unable to report for their execution. At first, I took no stock in the story. However, as the afternoon wore on and he did not appear, I began to believe that there might be some truth in what was being circulated. After dinner, I decided to find out from the warden.

Warden Deyo was nervously pacing the floor when I entered his office. I told him what I had heard, and inquired if he knew anything about it.

"Yes," he replied, "I've heard it, too. I haven't had a word from Davis, but I'm sure he'll be here. If he couldn't come, he'd have let me know before this."

"But suppose he doesn't show up?" I ventured. "What then?"

"Somebody else will have to do it."

"Who?"

The warden stopped walking, and sat down. "You could do it, couldn't you?" he asked.

His question startled me, and I did not answer immediately. For the first time in my life, I was faced with the possibility of performing an execution. I did not know what to say. While I believed that Davis would eventually arrive,

I realized that if he failed to do so and I replied affirmatively to the warden's question, I would be called upon to act as the executioner of the three men the following morning.

Finally, I said: "I don't believe I could do it, Warden. I've never seen an execution, and I wouldn't know what to do."

"There's really nothing to it," declared the warden. "With what you know about electricity, you wouldn't have any trouble at all. One of the guards who attends every execution could show you anything you didn't quite understand. Of course, if it's a case of not wanting to do the job, that's a different matter."

Both of us remained silent for several minutes. The warden was the first to speak.

"Suppose the Van Wormers had killed your father. Wouldn't you be willing to throw the switch on them then? Frankly, I don't relish this thing any more than you do. It's a nasty business, this taking men out and killing them. But it has to be done, and I suppose they've got it coming to them."

Warden Deyo rose from his chair, and started pacing up and down again.

"Those executions tomorrow have me worried," he confided. "The whole world is watching this case, and the slightest mishap will bring all kinds of criticism down on our heads. I wish the governor would do something, but I don't think he will. His wife has been begging him for the last few days to save the boys. I imagine he's more uneasy than I am."

At this point, Davis walked into the room. I do not know when I was ever so glad to see anybody. Warden Deyo told him of our fears, arid the executioner appeared much amused. Davis explained that the reason for his arrival at this hour was that he had taken a later train than usual, and it was delayed en route.

Walking home that night, I pondered whether I would have taken Davis' place at the controls had he failed to report in time for the executions. I came to the conclusion that I would have. I was, after all, in the prison service, and considered it my duty to comply with the warden's requests.

The next day dawned with threatening skies. When I arrived at the prison, I learned that the three youths had passed a sleepless night, tossing uneasily on their cots. It was the decision of Burton and Fred that Willis, the oldest but most nervous and distraught of the boys, should go to the chair first. Fred, the youngest, was to follow; then Burton, who it was believed could best endure those last terrifying minutes about which you and I can know little.

At 11.15 A.M., the bell sounded to start the engine. Thirty-five minutes later came the signal to cut off the current. Three men had paid with their lives for the one they had taken. I stopped the generator, changed the armature, and left the prison to return home for lunch.

My house was but two blocks from the prison, so it did not take me long to reach it. As I opened the front door, the bell of the old-fashioned wall telephone was ringing. My wife answered the call.

"It's for you," she said, handing me the receiver. "Whoever it is, is awfully excited about something."

The call was from Billy Roberts, a trusty assigned to duty in the power plant and about whom I will have more to say later.

"Come back!" he shouted. "Davis says to hurry! There's trouble!"

I dashed out of the house without a word to my wife, and was at the prison plant in less than three minutes. Davis was waiting for me.

"Get the engine going," he ordered. "One of the boys is alive. We've got to put him back in the chair." The executioner hastened to the death chamber.

Feverishly, I brought the power up to the required voltage. The signal came to turn on the current. A few minutes later, Davis appeared at the plant.

"Stop the engine," he said. "We won't need the current. He died before we got him in the chair."

I shut off the power, and went up to the death chamber. There I learned what had happened. The 1,700 volts which had coursed through the straining body of Fred Van Wormer, the youngest of the three murderers, had not killed him. Taken from the chair after the doctors had pronounced him dead, his body had been laid in an adjoining room to await the customary autopsy. A guard, Will Parsons, chanced in the room after the executions were over, and saw Fred's hand move and an eye flicker. He ran out of the room calling for the prison physician, who had already started to examine Willis and Burton.

"He moved!" Parsons yelled, pointing in the direction of the slab on which Fred lay. "I saw him move! We've got to do something quick!"

An immediate investigation proved that the guard was right. Fred's heart, larger than that of any other person electrocuted up to that time, was still beating, and he was alive. There was only one thing to do: put him in the chair again, and pass current through his body until he was dead.

It was a very much puzzled Davis who talked with me later about the incident. "I can't understand it," he said. "I gave him two shocks of the full current, and kept it on two minutes. The doctors were so sure he was dead I didn't bother with a third one. I wish now I had."

Not a word about Fred Van Wormer's brief survival reached outside the prison. Newspapers informed their readers that the three brothers went to the chair "without one unforeseen incident to mar the perfect and dignified' execution of the death penalty imposed by the trial court." Several did, however, mention the fact that when a group of some fifty long-termers saw the witnesses leaving the death house, they displayed their resentment at what had happened by hissing and uttering hideous shrieks. Demonstrations of this sort among convicts on execution days were not uncommon, and at times were difficult to check.

Superintendent Collins met me shortly afterward, and asked if I had witnessed the triple execution. I replied that

33

I had not, and explained the reason. He instructed me to accompany Davis to Sing Sing when the next execution was scheduled there. At this one, he told me, I was merely to observe how the state kills a man; at subsequent ones, I was to help Davis. But nothing was said about my ever being called upon to throw the switch. As one of Davis' assistants, I was to receive additional compensation. I accepted the assignment.

I PUT A MAN TO DEATH

The nine months following the deaths of the Van Wormers determined, to a large extent, the future course of my life. During this period, I helped Davis at a number of executions, each of which brought me a step closer to the time when I was to end a man's life at the state's bidding.

In mid-November of 1903, notice came from Warden Addison Johnson, of Sing Sing, that I was to report there for a scheduled execution. I informed my wife that I was going, and she raised no objection. She thought, as I did, that my role as Davis' assistant would be little more than that of an observer.

Executions at Sing Sing took place on Monday at six A.M. Leaving the power plant at Dannemora in care of trusted convicts, I entrained for Ossining on Saturday night. Arthur Neafie, who had worked with me at Avon and was now chief engineer at the penitentiary on the Hudson River, met me at the station on Sunday, and the two of us spent most of the day together. I also remained at his home overnight.

It was cold and dark the next morning when Neafie and I made our way down to the prison. Davis and Currier arrived a few minutes after five o'clock, and all of us immediately proceeded to the death chamber to get things ready. The electric chair was similar to the one in

Clinton Prison. Behind it was a booth containing the controls. In this enclosure, originally built to hide the executioner from view, Davis performed his duty.

While Currier busied himself with preparing the apparatus, Davis explained the entire operation in detail. "Watch closely all that goes on," he instructed, "and then you'll know exactly how it's done. It's really quite simple."

As the clock ticked off the few remaining minutes of the condemned man's life, guards and physicians came into the death chamber. Davis introduced me to all of them, and asked one of the officers, "What did the fellow back there do?" He nodded in the direction of the death cells.

"Oh, he had a quarrel with a woman because her husband wouldn't pay some money he owed him," answered the guard. "He shot her three times."

At five minutes of six, Davis and Currier took their positions by the chair. The executioner motioned me to a spot where I could watch his every move. Witnesses were ushered in and seated. The warden went after the doomed man.

The murderer, Carmine Gaimari, then entered, flanked by two black-robed priests. With unfaltering step, he walked directly to the electric chair and sat down. Guards strapped him in; Davis applied the head electrode, and Currier, the one on the leg. A black mask hid Gaimari's face. Davis moved to the booth, and his hand grasped the switch. The doctor gave the signal. Eighteen hundred volts—the greatest amount used at a Sing Sing execution up to that time—were sent through the slayer's body.

My eyes never left Davis as he alternately raised and lowered the current. Had I expected to find any indication that the grim task was difficult or repugnant to him, I would surely have been disappointed. He was just a person bent on doing his job well—nothing more.

Turning to me after Gaimari had been pronounced dead, Davis inquired, "Any questions?"

I replied that there were none.

On the way back to Dannemora, I tried to determine my reactions to the first execution I had witnessed. I discovered that there had not been any, except a sort of pity for the condemned man as he had walked into the room. I could not convince myself that I had actually been present at his death. It was all over so quickly, and I had been so engrossed in what Davis was doing that I had had little opportunity to experience the normal emotions of those who can see the occupant of the chair the entire time. Consequently, my first trip to Sing Sing had no particular effect on me.

A few days after I returned from Ossining, a unique election was held in New York State. The prisoners under sentence of death at Sing Sing picked a mayor. I read about it in the paper, and obtained more of the details on my next visit to the prison.

In December, 1902, those confined in Sing Sing's death house had chosen as their leader Arthur Flanagan, who had killed a prison keeper. Flanagan's execution the following spring had left the office vacant, and Albert T. Patrick, convicted of planning the murder of an eccentric old millionaire, had been selected for the unexpired term.

Patrick was an able lawyer. Besides preparing his own case for the Court of Appeals, he had aided the other condemned men in their efforts to get new trials. He had drafted Flanagan's letters for clemency to Governor Odell, which had been so strong that they won Flanagan a two weeks' reprieve.

So satisfactorily had Patrick served as mayor that he was unanimously re-elected on December 1, 1903, after another candidate had withdrawn from the race. When the balloting was over, the successful candidate made a short speech, in which he thanked his fellow unfortunates for the confidence they had in him, and assured them that he would endeavor to rule with fairness.

As "chief executive" of the death house, Patrick exercised quite some authority over the condemned men. His duties were described by the New York *World* as follows:

37

If two of the inmates want to play checkers, it is necessary for all the others to be quiet. In case the majority should object to a game, the question is referred to the mayor, whose decision is final. Absolute silence is necessary, because the two persons playing do not see each other nor can they play on one board. Each has a board marked on paper in his cell, and the moves are called off across the hall. It is the same with chess.

Whistling concerts are indulged in now and then, but only, when the mayor permits. All matters of etiquette and all points of law are passed upon by him.

At the time of this election, there were nine men in Sing Sing's death house. One of these was the first person I was to execute. Another was to do something to me in the death chamber that will always remain vivid in my memory. Patrick, incidentally, never went to the chair. His sentence was commuted three years later.

It fell to my lot to fasten the leg electrode on the first policeman to pay the supreme penalty in the electric chair. This occurred at Sing Sing on December 14, 1903. The doomed prisoner was William B. Ennis, a Brooklyn patrolman who had murdered his wife and attempted to kill his mother-in-law. In the hope of escaping electrocution, he had feigned insanity. For hours at a time, he would crouch in his cell with his chin almost touching his knees, and when taken out to be bathed and shaved, would hop on his toes instead of walking. Examinations by doctors revealed that he was shamming.

Just before the execution, Davis set me in the chair, rolled up my right trouser leg, and applied the lower electrode. "Now you put it on me," he directed. I followed his instructions, and he seemed satisfied that I knew how to do it.

I must confess that I was a bit nervous as Ennis strode unaided to the chair. But his brave demeanor calmed me. He looked on as I made the leg electrode firm. Some water from the head electrode trickled down the side of his face, and a guard whispered, "Sorry."

"Oh, I guess it won't harm me very much," Ennis replied with a half smile.

My work done, I stepped away, as did the others. Standing slightly toward the rear of the chair, I saw the body lurch against the straps when the deadly current struck it. I watched its movements as the voltage was lowered and increased. Sparks danced about the leg electrode part of the time. Grayish-blue smoke rose from the head, and a faint odor of burning flesh reached my nostrils. I felt slightly nauseated. I looked away from the chair, and noticed that Warden Johnson and several others had done likewise. For the first time, I had seen electricity kill a man whom I had helped prepare for death.

Ennis' courage had made my work easier that day— but I was not to be so fortunate the next time. In fact, the incident I am about to relate nearly caused me to quit as Davis' assistant.

Word was received shortly after the ex-policeman was in his grave that I was to go to Auburn Prison for the execution of Frank White, a mulatto. White had enticed his employer, an Oswego County farmer, into a cornfield, and fired several bullets into his back. Then he had hidden the body in a shock of corn.

On the morning that White was put to death, I met John Hulbert, who years later succeeded Davis as exe-cutioner. Hulbert was in charge of the prison's power plant then, and furnished current for the chair. He was short and stocky, and not the friendly type. I talked with him on all my visits to Auburn, but never saw him after he took over Davis' job.

In the death chamber, we were warned that White would be difficult. During his imprisonment, he had been quarrelsome, displaying violence on numerous occasions. On the day before Christmas, he had run amuck in the narrow confines of his cell. Latest reports from death row were that he had refused all spiritual help, and was in an extremely ugly mood. The prison authorities were preparing for any emergency.

Davis scoffed at the idea that he would have trouble with the mulatto. "When the time comes, he'll be just like all the rest," the executioner remarked. "There won't be any fight left in him. He'll be as meek as a lamb."

I have made similar statements many times upon being informed that I should expect a demonstration from the condemned person. And, except in one instance, my predictions have been correct. But Davis went wide of the mark' in this case.

Again my job was to apply the leg electrode. At the appointed hour, the door leading from the death cells into the execution chamber opened, and I saw a quaking, blubbering figure, supported on each side by a burly guard. The officers pushed him into the room. As his eyes fell upon the electric chair, he screamed in terror, and tried frantically to free himself from those gripping him.

"Don't kill me! Don't do it! Don't do it!" he cried.

The guards dragged the frightened man across the floor, and forced him into the chair. He continued moaning, and resisted attempts to adjust the straps. I bent down to fasten the lower electrode, but he kicked so vigorously that I had to appeal to a guard to hold the leg still. With his help, I managed to push up a piece of slit trouser, and attach the cold, wet electrode.

White struggled against his bonds, and mumbled incoherently until Davis threw the switch. Even then he tenaciously clung to life, six shocks being necessary before he was pronounced dead.

One of the physicians who listened with a stethoscope after the fourth contact and reported that White's heart was still beating was Dr. Ulysses B. Stein, of Buffalo. When the fifth shock was administered, he fainted and pitched forward from his front-row seat to the hard floor. I helped to carry the unconscious doctor from the death chamber into another room, where he was soon revived. This, together with White's behavior, and a gurgling in his throat while the current was on (caused by air escaping from the lungs), horrified many of the spectators. They fairly ran out into the open when permitted to leave.

White's execution disturbed me – so much so that I told Davis about it. I suggested that he get somebody else to take my place.

"That was a pretty bad one, I've got to admit," Davis commented. "It's the first time I've ever seen a fellow carry on the way he did. He was so scared I guess he didn't know what he was doing. But you don't get one like that very often. Most of them just walk in and don't say a word."

Davis urged me to continue as his assistant until he had fulfilled his agreement with the state. It would not be very long, he assured me, and then, if I wished, I could give up the work. Finally, I consented to go on; but fervently hoped that there would never be another execution as nerve-racking as White's.

Only two of the trusties who worked for me in the powerhouse at Dannemora escaped from prison. Billy Roberts, the convict who telephoned me at home after the Van Wormer execution, was one, and Jack Stewart, an older man, the other. They both made a dash for freedom on January 10, 1904.

Perhaps I should have suspected several days before the break that something was brewing. Roberts, normally a talkative man, was quiet and sullen. Stewart seemed to be on edge, and also had little to say. The idea that the two were plotting to escape never entered my mind, for I knew Roberts had only three more months of a ten-year sentence to serve.

The two set a Sunday when I was not on duty to carry out their scheme. At ten o'clock that night, they climbed over the wall without anybody's seeing them. Although there was three feet of snow in that vicinity, they walked to Plattsburg, where they took shelter in the stables on the county fair grounds.

But even escaped convicts have to eat and drink. So, after four days of hiding, the men came out in search of food and water. A farmer had his wife cook them a big dinner, and gave them some pork to take along. After they had departed, the farmer wondered whether they were the prisoners being sought by the authorities. He telephoned the police, and described the two who had been his guests. A few hours later, Roberts and Stewart were caught and returned to finish out their sentences.

Roberts was reassigned to the plant shortly afterward. I asked him why he had escaped since his life behind bars was nearly ended. He explained that Stewart was determined to break out, irrespective of the consequences; and insisted that he do the same. Rather than remain behind and be punished for failing to disclose Stewart's plans to the attendants, he had preferred to accompany him. Fortunately for Roberts, the warden understood why he had joined in the plot, and no charges were brought against him. He was freed when his original time was up.

My first experience in placing the head electrode on a person about to die was at the execution of Thomas Tobin, who was found guilty of an unusually brutal murder. Sing Sing guards called him the worst prisoner ever confined in that institution. He was abusive to his keepers and to the other inmates of the death house.

What annoyed Tobin more than anything else was the fact that he had built the very death house in which he was incarcerated. He had served a previous term for burglary, and it was while he was imprisoned that New York State had changed the method of capital punishment from hanging to death by electrocution. The legislature also had ordered that in the future all condemned men should occupy separate cells. As Tobin was a mason by trade and possessed some knowledge of architecture, the warden selected him to prepare plans for the new building and to superintend its erection. He had accepted this assignment eagerly, and, unknown to anyone except a few of the convicts on the job with him, had constructed a secret passage leading to a sewer which ran into the Hudson River.

"You don't think I'd do all this work without getting something out of it for Tom Tobin, do you?" he said to them.

Soon after the completion of the death house, Tobin made a getaway through the sewer. Eighteen months elapsed before he was captured and returned to prison. He went to New York City following his formal discharge, and there committed the crime for which he was condemned to die.

From the minute he entered the death house, he constantly cursed his ill fortune. "To think," he would rave, "that I should have built this place for myself! I built my own tomb, that's what I did!"

During the month immediately preceding his execution on March 14, 1904, Tobin pretended to believe that there were rats in his cell. He would race around as though chasing them. His guards thought he was insane; but a commission appointed by the governor to examine him reported that he was merely trying to escape the chair.

Davis apprised me on the morning of Tobin's execution as to what my duties would be that day. No sooner had he told me than, as in the case of White, we heard that Tobin was behaving rather badly, and might not be easy to handle in the death chamber. I steeled myself for the worst. But he offered no resistance as he was led to the chair, and I soon had the head electrode on him. Until the switch was thrown, he kept repeating a prayer taught him by his mother when he was a child.

Execution days were almost invariably bad ones among the inmates. This was especially true at Clinton Prison. The knowledge that a fellow prisoner was about to die in the chair bred unrest, and the convicts grew morose and ugly. Some were unable to do their work properly until the electrocution had taken place. They were continually asking such questions as "Is it all over yet?", "Was everything all right?", "Was he game?" More guards were always on duty on these occasions, and men were stationed at regular intervals along the route of the wire strung from the power plant to the death hose to prevent it from being cut.

As I have mentioned before, noon was the time set for executions at Dannemora. At this hour, convicts from the shops filed past the plant on the way to their cells for lunch. This made me uneasy – and never more so than when Allan Mooney was put to death on May 3, 1904.

Mooney had killed two women and wounded a man at Saranac Lake, New York, in the winter of 1902. For nearly a year, he had awaited his turn to walk "the last mile." He had sobbed as the three Van Wormer brothers went to their doom. One of them–Burton–as he stepped from his cell on the way to the chair, had called: "Good-by, Mooney. I hope you won't have to go like this." Mooney had hoped so, too.

It was a warm day when Mooney died, and I kept the doors and windows of the powerhouse open. While the execution was going on, convicts tramped by. They peered in at the generator, and glared at me. They knew full well that I was sending current to the death chamber for the purpose of ending Mooney's life.

Although guards were near by, fear gripped me. I was not afraid of what the convicts might do to me so much as I was of how simple it would be for a group of them to break line, dash into the building, overpower the few of us in the plant, and damage the engines before help could arrive. This would have caused consternation in the death chamber–perhaps even suffering for the condemned man. I tried to appear unconcerned, at the same time keeping an eye on the marching men. There was no disturbance, however; and I breathed more easily when the signal sounded to turn off the current.

That afternoon I spoke to Warden Deyo of my fears. Whether this had anything to do with it, I do not know; but all executions at Dannemora after that day were held at six o'clock in the morning while the convicts were still in their cells. It was a great relief to me, and I think Davis welcomed the change.

Little did I dream on that night the following June when I boarded the train for Ossining that before I returned, I would actually have killed a man whom the law had decreed must die. So far as I knew, I was merely on my way to assist at a double execution.

Two men—Albert Koepping and Oscar Borgstrom—were to sit in Sing Sing's chair on the same day. In a jealous rage, the former had murdered a Port Jervis merchant, and the latter had slain his wife. Both had fought desperately to escape the supreme penalty, but were unsuccessful.

I saw in a paper on the train that the supposedly unlucky number thirteen figured prominently in one of the cases. Borgstrom had committed his crime on April 13, 1903; he was to be executed on the thirteenth day of the month, and there were thirteen men in the condemned cells awaiting death. I am not superstitious, so what I read did not bother me.

As on other occasions, I spent Sunday at the Neafie home. Neafie was the only one who referred to the forthcoming executions. He mentioned the fact that Koepping had issued a sensational statement protesting his innocence.

"Koepping says that the man's own wife did the killing," Neafie told me.

"But I thought he confessed," I remarked.

"Yeah, he did confess, but now he says he did it because she promised to testify at the trial that he shot her husband in self-defense. He insists he didn't have a thing to do with the actual murder."

I could not help wondering whether Koepping was innocent after all. Perhaps I would have thought even more about it had I known at the time that I was to be his executioner.

Upon my arrival at the death chamber the next day, Davis walked over to me and unceremoniously announced: "Bob, I want you to throw the switch on one of the fellows this morning."

He watched my reaction. I am sure it was exactly what he had expected. His statement came as such a surprise that I was unable to reply. Davis realized this, and hastened to explain why he had made the request.

"You see, Bob," he said, "I've got to train two men to be executioners. That means that, before I'm through, both of them have to do the job at least once. Currier has already done his, and now it's your turn. I'll be right by you all the time, and you won't have a thing to worry about. You can take care of the first one."

At last, I managed to say, "All right."

Then followed final instructions, which I only half heard. I pretended to examine the electrodes and chair, seeking to hide from Davis and the others the fact that I, who had been comparatively cool and efficient heretofore when only an "accomplice" to the state's killings, was now perturbed as I faced the ordeal of throwing the switch.

After the witnesses were seated, Davis tested the chair with a board of lights. I stood immediately to the right of the death seat, the head electrode in my hand. I was trembling. Davis noticed this, and said, "Steady, Bob, steady."

Koepping was brought in, and walked firmly to the chair. As he sat down, he reiterated his earlier statement that he was expiating the crime of another. I placed the electrode on his head. I could feel him shudder as several drops of water ran down the back of his neck. Next I went over to the switch ten feet away. Davis was there, and he put his hand on my shoulder reassuringly. I reached out for the switch, and my right hand closed around it.

While I waited for the signal, I heard the nervous cough of one of the witnesses. There was the shifting of feet, and a terse, quiet word spoken by an official. My temples throbbed.

The prison physician then gave the signal by a wave of his hand. I glanced at the chair to be sure that nobody was standing too near it. "Now," whispered Davis. I threw the switch, and the condemned man stiffened under the straps. In a few seconds, Davis said, "Cut it down." I reduced the amount of current, and the body slumped. Finally, after the necessary number of shocks, it was decided that justice had been done. I went over and unfastened the head electrode. What had once been a living man was removed from the chair, and wheeled into the autopsy room. I had killed him.

On the second prisoner who was to die that day, I was to apply the leg electrode. I felt that this would be much easier than throwing the switch. But I was entirely unaware of what was in store for me.

The door opened, and Borgstrom, fair-haired and huge in frame, entered the death chamber. His face was set as if it were stone, and he looked straight ahead. Without a word, he proceeded to the chair. A gentle push from a guard and he took his seat. I bent down to attach the electrode to the big man's right leg.

As I made the electrode firm, I followed an irresistible impulse. I glanced up into the impassive face of the condemned man, and my eyes caught the burning, baleful glare of his. I saw fear registered there. But there also was hate—uncompromising hate for those who were doing the same thing to him that he had done to his wife. However, this killing was legal, because it was ordered and approved by the state.

It was the first time I had ever looked into the eyes of an individual on the brink of eternity. The blaze of those blue eyes held mine. I was as though hypnotized. I could feel perspiration on my forehead. A strange sensation passed over me, and I could not move. Neither could I take my eyes from his. I heard somebody say, "Hurry." Somehow I knew this meant me. By dint of actual physical effort, I closed my eyes for a second. When I opened them, I did not look up. I had broken the spell. Quickly I completed my task and turned away. I staggered to a corner of the room, where I remained until the execution was over. I was weak as the witnesses shuffled out of the chamber.

Since that morning, I have thrown the switch that has sent three hundred and eighty-seven people into the next world. But never again have I looked into the eyes of another condemned person.

After all had departed except Davis, Currier, and me, Warden Johnson came back into the death chamber and invited us to have breakfast with him. We accepted and accompanied him to his home. I was still nervous, and did not eat very much.

Eventually, the conversation got around to the executions. The warden expressed satisfaction with the efficient manner in which they had been handled. He added that several witnesses had remarked about the humaneness of the electric chair.

"I think Bob did all right today, don't you, Warden?" asked Davis.

"I certainly do," answered the prison head. "But why did you have him execute the first man? Wouldn't it have been better if he had done the second one?"

"On the contrary. If he'd waited, he might have lost his nerve. Once he'd done that, I could never have gotten him to throw the switch."

"Perhaps you're right. I hadn't thought of it that way."

When I returned to Clinton Prison, Edward Lewis, a death house guard who applied the leg electrode at all executions there, asked me how I had made out at Sing Sing. I told him that I had executed a man, and related my unusual experience with Borgstrom. He smiled as I gave him the details.

"I've never told this to anybody before," Lewis confided, "but the same thing happened to me with one of the Van Wormers. I looked up at Burton while I was putting the leg electrode on him, and he hypnotized me. Believe me, I was scared. I didn't know what to do. I couldn't look away, and I couldn't budge. As soon as Davis put the mask over the fellow's eyes, I was all right again. The P. K. [principal keeper] told me afterward that I acted like I was drunk. I didn't have the nerve to tell him what really happened. He'd have thought I was crazy."

Although it soon got around among the guards and the convicts working for me at the plant that I had performed an execution, I noticed no change in their attitude toward me. I kept the knowledge from my wife that I had acted as executioner, because she could not have reconciled herself then to her husband's part in the grisly business of legal death. Not until years later did she learn that as Davis' assistant I had been more than a witness. The news brought no comment from her.

A VISIT WITH THE CONDEMNED

During my association with Davis, our relationship was as agreeable as was possible under the circumstances. Only once did he reprimand me, and that, oddly enough, was not while we were on duty. It occurred in a New York City restaurant.

Fear of being recognized constantly dogged Davis' footsteps. I have known him to go miles out of his way to avoid being seen. One time he went up the west side of the Hudson River instead of the east, crossed over, and arrived at Sing Sing from the north—all to escape possible detection.

There were two reasons for Davis' actions. One was that he had received many threats against his life, presumably from friends or relatives of those whom he had executed or who were under sentence of death. The other was his dislike of being pointed out as "the man who throws the switch."

Twice after executions at Sing Sing, he and I spent a few hours together in New York City. On the second of these occasions, we decided to have dinner at a popular eating place not far from Times Square. I scanned the menu and asked, "What are you going to have, Davis?"

For what seemed a long time, he did not reply. Instead, he glanced cautiously around the room to determine whether anyone had heard me. He reminded me of a hunted animal that had been cornered. Finally, he admonished: "Don't ever call my name when you talk to me. Somebody might hear you and recognize me."

"Davis is a common enough name," I argued, "and wouldn't mean a thing to most folks. There are thousands of Davises in the country."

"Maybe," he agreed, "but there's only one who does the work I do. So forget who I am when we're out."

Realizing how sensitive he was on this point, I respected his wish, and never again addressed him by name in public. But even then he did not appear entirely at ease if people were near us.

Davis ordinarily traveled by himself to and from executions. As we thought he might be lonely, Mrs. Elliott and I often invited him to dine with us when he came to Dannemora. He thoroughly enjoyed these meals, and complimented my wife on her cooking. While Mrs. Elliott was doing the dishes, he and I would sometimes chat about his work, of which he would speak freely to me. One night we talked about two of his most famous cases.

"She was one of the coolest people I've ever executed," Davis said of Mrs. Martha Place, the first woman to be electrocuted for murder. "She didn't cause us a bit of trouble in the death chamber. We waited until she was in the chair before clipping the spot on her head. It was so quick I don't think she noticed it at all. Her eyes were closed, and I heard her say, 'God save me.' The guards and witnesses acted more upset than she did."

"How did you feel about throwing the switch on a woman?" I inquired.

"To tell you the truth, Bob, I was pretty worried at first," he confessed. "I thought about it a lot. The idea of killing a woman just didn't seem right. But after a while I decided that simply because she was a woman didn't make her different from any other murderer. Besides, somebody had to execute her, and that was my job."

Defiance to the very end marked the passing of Leon F. Czolgosz, the youthful anarchist who fatally shot President McKinley at the Pan-American Exposition in

Buffalo in 1901, Davis informed me. The assassin's last words were to the effect that he had no regrets whatever for the crime which had shocked the nation, but was sorry that he was unable to see his father before going to the chair.

"I'm sure Czolgosz was disappointed because more people weren't there when he died," Davis added. "He wanted a large crowd, and intended to make a speech; but Superintendent Collins wouldn't allow it. The execution was over in less than four minutes, and was as successful as any I've ever had."

An inmate of Clinton Prison's death house, shortly before he walked "the last mile," asked a guard to bring the executioner to his cell. "I'd like to see what the guy who's going to finish me looks like," he explained. This unusual request was communicated to Davis in the death chamber, who, much to the surprise of the prison attendants, consented.

As he stood in front of the condemned man, with only iron bars separating the two, the prisoner eyed him appraisingly.

"Now that you've seen me, what do you think of me?" Davis asked.

"Boy, you're the homeliest son-of-a-gun I've ever seen," was the murderer's only comment.

The prisoner was led to the chair half an hour later. Before sitting down, he turned to Davis and remarked, "I ain't changed my mind about that mug of yours."

I heard a story about Davis several years ago that is hard to believe. Yet it was related to me by the very person to whom he is supposed to have made the astonishing statement. Otherwise, I should not have lent any credence to the tale, or considered repeating it here.

It seems that Davis went to a notary public to have his bill to the state sworn to. The notary managed to engage him in conversation, during which he asked many questions. He wanted to know, for instance, whether Davis would execute anybody at all who was sentenced to die by electricity. Davis replied that he would.

"Suppose the fellow was your own son–then what?" continued the inquisitive notary.

"That wouldn't make any difference," the executioner bluntly declared. "If he committed murder, he'd deserve the chair. And I'd do my duty."

Being acquainted with Davis as intimately as I was for a number of years, I am convinced that had he been faced with the ordeal of executing a friend or relative, he would have refused to serve. Moreover, I doubt seriously whether the warden would have asked him to officiate under such circumstances.

One thing I do know about Davis: he was obsessed with the idea that somebody was going to take his job away from him. In addition to New York State, he was the executioner for New Jersey and Massachusetts. Shortly after I had thrown the switch for the first time, he remarked that New Jersey might send for me to perform an execution.

"If they do, and you go, don't do the work any cheaper than I would," he said.

However, New Jersey did not approach me until twenty-two years later, and Davis never explained why he had brought up the subject. Perhaps he thought that the state regarded his fee as too high, and might try to obtain the services of another whose charge would be less.

Had it not been for the gravity of the occasion, an incident occurred at one of the last executions I attended while working with Davis that might have been amusing. After Nelson Bogganio had received the final shock in Auburn's electric chair on the morning of December 13, 1904, Dr. Gerin, the prison physician, mistaking a witness for a fellow practitioner, handed him a stethoscope. This man, who was a policeman, had never seen an execution or a stethoscope before. He apparently thought it was part of a witness' duty to do whatever the doctor did.

When the prison physician walked over to the chair to examine its occupant, the policeman followed him. Fixing the instrument to his ears, he applied the other end somewhere near the region of the condemned man's heart and listened carefully. He solemnly announced that he could hear nothing.

"I pronounce this man dead," declared Dr. Gerin.

"I pronounce this man dead," repeated the policeman.

Nobody quite realized what had happened, for it is not unusual for visiting physicians to be present at executions. But the policeman was very much embarrassed when he later learned that he had acted in the place of a doctor who had traveled some distance to participate in the execution.

Shortly after this, there was an opening as chief engineer at the Rochester Industrial School, a New York State reformatory for boys. As my wife's parents, as well as relatives of mine, lived in the vicinity, and the job would mean a promotion for me, I took the examination. On February 1, 1905, I was appointed to the position, and moved my family to Rochester.

At the same time, I stopped attending executions with Davis. He expressed regret that I would no longer help him, and wished me the best of luck in my new work. John Hulbert, the chief engineer at Auburn Prison of whom I have spoken before, succeeded me as Davis' assistant.

A month after I had gone to Rochester, a Lewis E. Lawes was employed as guard at Clinton Prison. He was above the average prison attendant in intelligence and resourcefulness—a fact soon recognized by all who came to know him.

"He won't stay in this business very long," they predicted.

But they were wrong. Lawes did remain, and later became warden of Sing Sing Prison.

Lawes and I first met at Dannemora shortly before he left for Auburn, where he was also a guard. He impressed me as possessing unusual ability, and I thought then how much better the prison service would be were there more men like him in it. Little did I suspect that some day I would act as executioner at a penitentiary of which he was warden.

I was not particularly satisfied at the industrial school. Consequently, when Principal Keeper James Fulton, of Clinton Prison, urged me to return to the penitentiary, I welcomed the opportunity. I was made chief engineer, and, as such, supervised the plumbing, heating, and lighting of the prison.

Major changes in prison life at Dannemora took place about this time, most of them during the administration of Warden Deyo. Among them were the abolishment of the lock step and the discarding of striped suits for plain gray ones. A mess hall was constructed so that the convicts would not have to eat in their cells, and porcelain dishes were substituted for tin. Electric lights replaced kerosene lamps in all cells. Most important was the establishment of the parole system. A man who worked for me at the plant was the first to be paroled from Clinton Prison.

Exercise periods were also instituted. Trouble was anticipated the first morning when all of the convicts were turned loose in the yard for exercise. The guards were alert for any suspicious move. Even the warden was uneasy as he watched the milling crowd from one of the windows. But there was no disorder, and at the call, each man was back with his company.

These changes had a very definite effect on the convicts. They became more hopeful, more optimistic as to the future. They were less sullen and resentful against society. They proved easier to handle. Demonstrations and attempts to escape grew fewer. While the prison authorities still had a great deal to learn about the best way to treat prisoners, a step in the right direction had been taken.

An experience I shall never forget was a visit I had with a condemned man on the night before he was executed. We talked for nearly an hour, and I believe it was our conversation that enabled him to go to his death with fortitude.

The prisoner was Leslie Coombs, a youth of twenty. Before he committed the murder that landed him in Clinton Prison's death house, he had been convicted of two other crimes. He had served time in the Rochester Industrial School for burglary, and was sent to Dannemora in 1907 for a like offense. Not long after entering the prison, he was made a trusty, and was assigned to the powerhouse. There was something about the boy that I liked, and we became friends.

For some reason, Leslie did not mix with the other convicts. When with me, he was talkative, and told me of his early life and his plans for the future. Unfortunately, he was weak-willed and easily led, which probably accounted for his misdeeds.

At least once that I recall, Leslie accompanied me to the death chamber. He saw the electric chair, and commented about its gruesome appearance. He also helped me at the plant when I was furnishing current for executions. Yet these things failed to keep his finger from a trigger shortly afterward.

On the morning Leslie was released from prison, I chanced to be at the railroad station, and ran into him. He was the happiest man in the world that day. We chatted as he anxiously awaited the arrival of the train.

"Behave yourself now that you're out," I counseled him.

"Don't worry, I will," he replied. "No more of this prison stuff for me. I've had enough."

I believed he really meant what he said. As the train started, he waved good-by, and I never expected to lay eyes on him again.

But apparently it was not Leslie's nature to stay out of trouble. Less than forty-eight hours after his discharge, he held up and robbed a man on a lonely road in St. Lawrence County, New York. Realizing that his victim recognized him, he shot the man. The law soon caught up with Leslie, and he was speedily convicted. His execution was set for February 16, 1909—only five weeks after he had been sentenced.

Two days before he was scheduled to die, I learned from guards that he had had no visitors, and did not expect any. Friends and relatives had entirely deserted him. Except for his lawyer, he had nobody on the outside fighting for him. I could not help feeling sorry for the lonely youth, who happened to be the only occupant of the death house at the time.

That noon I talked to my wife about Leslie. I suggested that he might like to see me, and she was of the same opinion. She even offered to prepare a home-cooked supper for him. Back at the prison, I sought out the principal keeper, and told him what I had in mind.

"If Coombs is willing, I think it would be a good idea," said the P. K. "He's been terribly nervous for the past week, and seeing you might do some good. I'll speak to him."

Word reached me at the power plant later that Leslie would be glad for me to visit him. The next day, Mrs. Elliott fixed a meal of roast chicken, mashed potatoes, carrots and peas, coffee, and apple pie. I added some cigarettes of his favorite brand.

An hour after I had eaten dinner that night, I took the basket of food down to the death house. Leslie seemed pleased that I had come.

"Here's a little something Mrs. Elliott sent you," I said, handing him the basket.

"Thanks," he replied. When he saw what it contained, he commented, "I guess you must've told her I like chicken."

While he was eating, I tried to bolster him up by talking about the convicts he knew at the powerhouse. However, he preferred to discuss what was going to happen to him the next morning. He wanted to know if there was any likelihood that the governor would intervene.

"No, Leslie, I'm afraid there's no hope," I told him. "You've made a serious mistake, and now you've got to pay for it."

"Yes, I guess so," he agreed, "but it'll be awfully tough. Will it hurt any?"

I assured him that there would be no pain. "The hardest part will be the going in. After that, it'll be over before you know it."

"Where will you be when I go in?" he asked.

"Down at the plant. But I'll be thinking about you and praying for you all the time."

Leslie remarked that he could not understand why he had followed a life of crime. The murder especially puzzled him, he said.

"Don't ask yourself why you did it," I advised him. "You'll never know, and it's far better not to think about it. Make your peace with God, and nothing else will matter."

This thought seemed to comfort him, and he asked many questions pertaining to religion. I answered him as best I could. Then he said, "I won't be scared tomorrow."

Leslie and I talked until he had finished his meal. He had, in spite of the strain, eaten most of it. When the guard appeared at the cell in response to my summons, Leslie firmly clasped my hand in both of his, and again expressed appreciation for the supper.

"Is there anything else I can do for you?" I asked.

"No, nothing." He turned away, but not quickly enough to hide a tear. It was with a heavy heart that I left the death house.

Although I took a long walk before returning home, I found it difficult to fall asleep. I thought of Leslie tossing restlessly on his cell cot, realizing that death was only a few hours away. Try as hard as I might, I could not get him out of my mind.

The next morning when the ammeter at the plant registered seven and a half amperes, I knew that Leslie's worldly troubles were ended. I offered a short prayer as I went about my work. As soon as the signal sounded to shut off the current, I hastened to the death chamber.

"How did everything go?" I inquired of Davis.

"Fine," replied the executioner. "He didn't act the least bit frightened. He walked straight to the chair, and sat down without saying a word. He seemed in a hurry to get it over with."

I was glad that I had visited Leslie the night before. I felt that, perhaps, I had helped to make his last torturous hours more endurable.

The next four years were more or less uneventful. However, there was an official investigation, which resulted in a change of wardens at Clinton Prison in 1911. In May of the same year, our second daughter, Gertrude, was born. I was kept very busy at the prison, but only a few executions took place there during that period. Months frequently passed without a single one.

According to my records, the last man to be put to death at Dannemora was Frederick A. Poulin. His execution on February 12, 1913, left the death house without an occupant. From then on, all electrocutions in New York State were held at Sing Sing, and this was a tremendous relief to all of us. When the chair was removed from Clinton Prison's death chamber, it was placed in the guard room. Even though it was no longer in use, curious visitors to the penitentiary insisted on seeing and sitting in it.

As Davis was getting on in years, he retired in 1914, spending the rest of his days in seclusion. During the twenty-odd years he served as society's agent of death, he executed approximately two hundred and forty convicted murderers, two of whom were women. Hulbert, having been trained for the job by Davis, was his logical successor.

The Reverend George Belanger, the Catholic chaplain at Clinton Prison while I was there, did more, perhaps, to bring peace and comfort into the bleak sector of the world's sorrow in which he served than any other person I have known. Although hating capital punishment, the saintly, white-haired priest strove to convince each condemned person that to give up his life willingly would mean the regaining of it hereafter.

One night as I was entering the prison, I met Father Belanger. On his kindly face was the saddest expression I had ever seen. I inquired as to what was troubling him.

"I can't get him to make his peace with God," he said of the man who was to be executed the following morning. "He is still defiant against the laws of God and man. I'm afraid he is going out into the next world alone."

An hour and a half later, I saw Father Belanger again. There were tears in his eyes, but a wonderful smile lighted his tired face.

"He is all right now," the clergyman told me. "His heart has softened and he has asked forgiveness. And I know he is sincere. Now he will not be alone when your current is turned on tomorrow."

Everybody at the prison, including the convicts, were anxious to do anything they could for Father Belanger. When, therefore, in the fall of 1914, he wanted an imported statue of Saint Joseph placed in the tower of his church in Dannemora, Warden John F. Trombley readily complied with his request that I do this job. I selected two trusted convicts to help me.

No men ever did a job more enthusiastically than those two prisoners. I believe they enjoyed every minute of it, and were sorry when the work was finished. While there was every opportunity for them to escape, I doubt that such a thought entered their minds. They were too eager to satisfy the gentle priest for whom they had the greatest respect and admiration.

During the two years which followed, I was on call day and night. The prison began selling current to the village, and I was needed at the plant a great deal of the time. Inmates operated the boiler and engine rooms, but the equipment was so inadequate for the demands that trouble often arose with which they could not cope.

However, I was extremely fortunate in having good workers at the plant. Most were serious-minded, and several looked upon the assignment as an opportunity to obtain knowledge about electricity. Jobs in the plant were

60

always sought after. In December, 1916, I received the following note from a prisoner:

I spoke to you recently in regards to a position in the powerhouse, and you told me to send you my name and number. As I wish to learn all I possibly can while I am serving my time, I trust that you may be able to give me a chance.

A vacancy occurred several weeks later, and I suggested that it be filled by this man. He was transferred to the engine room, where he proved a faithful assistant and an adept pupil. Upon being released from prison, he followed the trade of an electrician.

Clinton Prison had several baseball teams. I managed the one representing the engineering department, and a convict by the name of Kelly coached the prison band team. Keen rivalry existed between the two groups, which during the summer played five innings nearly every afternoon.

Whenever an application was made for a place in the engineering department, I casually inquired whether the man was a good ball player. If he was, and possessed the other necessary qualifications, I recommended him for the job. In this way, I built up a strong team, which won most of the games.

Kelly discovered one day that a convict from the cotton shop was playing with my boys. As the fellow was an exceptionally good second baseman, Kelly got the warden to sign a paper forbidding the man to play on my team because he was not in the powerhouse. I told the principal keeper of my loss, and he said he would see what he could do about it. That same day the convict was transferred to the plant, thereby making him eligible for the engineering department team. Kelly never complained again.

With America's entrance in the World War, many left the prison service to do their bit. Being past the enlistment age, I applied for service at the Brooklyn Navy Yard. Notice came early in June of 1918 for me to report for duty, and I did electrical work aboard ships until the

Armistice. My family moved to Richmond Hill, Long Island, that September, and we established our present home.

For about two and a half years following the war, I was chief engineer at the Woman's Hospital in New York City. Then my son, Robert, and I went into the electrical contracting business, in which we are still engaged.

It was rumored in the fall of 1925 that Hulbert had informed friends that he intended to resign as executioner the next summer, when he would be eligible for a pension. His health was poor, and his eyesight was failing, it was said. Once, a few minutes before he was to execute two men, he had collapsed in Sing Sing's death chamber. Dr. Amos O. Squire, the prison physician, administered stimulants, and Hulbert was able to perform the executions, which had been delayed by his sinking spell. He spent a week in the prison hospital recuperating from the illness.

As time passed, Hulbert became depressed. Death house guards have told me that, toward the end, he was given to fits of violent temper. He even refused to carry out orders. As he was preparing the chair at one of his last executions, he was handed a set of new electrodes which the warden wanted put on the condemned man. Hulbert replied that he had his own, and would use them. On being told that he must follow the warden's instructions, he picked up the new electrodes and hurled them across the room. He had his way that night.

"Sing Sing Executioner Quits Suddenly; Lawes May Have to Put Two to Death Himself," said a headline on the front page of my copy of The New York Times on Sunday, January 17, 1926. The story announced that, although there were nine occupants of the condemned cells scheduled to die within the month—two that coming Thursday night—Hulbert had unexpectedly resigned. The man who had put to death one hundred and twenty people in twelve years had given no reason for his sudden decision.

"Unless another man is found," the newspaper added, "Warden Lewis Lawes, under the statutes, must act as executioner."

For the first time since the introduction of the electric chair, New York State was without a man to throw the switch.

THE JOB IS MINE

Announcement of Hulbert's resignation as Sing Sing's executioner immediately brought Warden Lawes many applications for the post. They came by letter, wire, and telephone, and several individuals appeared in person at the prison. I believe there were close to a hundred men who were willing–and even anxious–to do the state's killing for a fee.

One of these was an electrician who lived only a block from me and was employed directly across the street from my home. I was not acquainted with him then; but a year or so after I had become the executioner, he called at the house, and wanted to act as my assistant when I put condemned prisoners to death.

Warden Lawes, in answer to questions, told the press that obtaining a person to take Hulbert's place was a great responsibility. "I can find a lot of morbid fellows to do the work," he said, "but the thing is to find a man with technical skill." He felt that this important task required a proficient, sure-handed electrician–a man qualified by training and experience. The warden revealed that he would first offer the place to all eligibles on the prison staff, and if they declined it, he would then seek an outsider.

The idea that I apply for the job was suggested by an ex-convict who had been in the powerhouse at Dannemora while I was there and whom I was trying to help by employing him in my electrical contracting business. He pointed out to me, on the morning following the news of Hulbert's unexpected action, that I was the logical one to serve as the state's executioner. In fact, he urged me to seek the appointment. When he saw that I was not seriously considering his proposal, he continued:

"The warden's in a spot. I guess he can get any number of guys who'd jump at the chance; but what he needs is somebody like you. You've done the work before, and know what it's all about. You ought to get in touch with him right away."

The more I thought about it, the more I realized that there was something to what this man said. The very purpose of Davis' instructing me in how to perform an execution was to meet just such an emergency as this. Moreover, with the exception of Hulbert, I was the only living man in New York State who had thrown the switch. I concluded that the least I could do was to offer my services to Warden Lawes.

That noon I talked the matter over with members of my family. I explained that I regarded it as a duty to communicate with the warden, and would do so unless they objected. My wife said nothing for a while, and then: "I don't like it; but if you think you should do it, go ahead." My son, Robert, and daughter, Frances, gave their approval.

I wrote Warden Lawes later in the day to the effect that I would be available should he be unsuccessful in obtaining someone entirely satisfactory. I advised him of my previous connection with the prison service and of my duties as Davis' assistant.

For two days after I had sent the letter, the newspapers devoted considerable space to the unprecedented situation at Sing Sing. Two men, Ambrose Ross and John Slattery, were scheduled to die in the electric chair that Thursday night for the murder of a bond clerk during a bank robbery at Bellmore, Long Island. Adding to the warden's strain were the critical illness of Mrs. Lawes and the absence from duty of Principal Keeper Thomas McInerney, who was in a hospital recuperating from an operation. McInerney, ordinarily in charge of the execution squad, took care of many of the details.

The expected reply from Warden Lawes failed to arrive in Wednesday morning's mail. Believing that my letter might not have reached the prison, and realizing that the time was growing short, I telephoned the warden. At his request, I went to Ossining that afternoon for an interview.

I was questioned by the warden and a representative from the General Electric Company. My answers soon convinced them that I was entirely familiar with the operation of the death chair. It was then suggested that I accompany the electrical expert and Chief Engineer John J. Shanahan to the execution chamber to inspect the apparatus.

While we were walking to the death house, a convict hailed me from a shop window. "Hello, Bob!" he shouted. "What are you doing up here?" The prisoner was a man who had worked for me in the power plant at Dannemora, and had also served time in other penitentiaries. He was one of the kind who simply cannot stay out of trouble.

"Just looking the place over," I replied. "You certainly get around, don't you?"

"Yeah," he said. "I'd hate to pass any of 'em up. They might feel slighted." He laughed heartily, and went on with his work.

Inside the death chamber, I was shown the electric chair, and everything was explained to me. I remarked that the apparatus, while more modern, differed little from that in use when I was at Clinton Prison. We then left the place.

For a reason that I do not know, we returned to the warden's office by another route. We passed through "the little green door" (which is not green at all) into the section of the death house where the condemned are kept. I saw Ross, who was conversing in low tones with a visitor. He did not glance up as we went by, nor did the other inmates pay much attention to us. Guards were the only people to whom we spoke on our way through the cheerless building. At no time since then have I been in that part of a prison.

Apparently satisfied that I was qualified for the work, Warden Lawes telephoned Superintendent of Prisons James L. Long that he thought the right man had been found. He explained to me that the state paid $150 for each person executed, and instructed me to report the next night for my first assignment.

As Warden Lawes was driving to New York City to see his wife in a hospital there, he invited the General Electric representative, Shanahan, and me to ride along with him. It was while on this trip that the warden suggested that my identity remain a secret, and that I shun all publicity. If the public were unaware of my connection with Sing Sing, my family and I would be spared the annoyance to which my predecessors had been subjected, he said. The idea appealed to me, and I agreed.

My wife had little to say when she learned that I had been chosen as Hulbert's successor. Her only comment was that she had hoped somebody else would be se- lected. She shared Warden Lawes' opinion that it would be better all around if my name were not linked with executions. We decided that only a few of our most intimate and trusted friends should be told. We also thought it wise to keep the truth from Gertrude, who was in her early teens and probably would not have understood.

During the day, Governor Alfred E. Smith had commuted Slattery's sentence to life imprisonment, and declared that he would not intervene in behalf of Ross. Worry over whether everything would go off without a hitch kept me awake part of the night; but I finally convinced myself that my fears were groundless. After all, I had acted in such a capacity before.

I took the train for Sing Sing late the next afternoon for what I believed was to be my first case as New York's official executioner. Upon my arrival at the prison, I was informed that a State Supreme Court order had prolonged Ross' life another twenty-four hours. My services, therefore, would not be needed that night. I breathed more easily as I walked out of the prison. My wife was glad, also, when I told her what had happened.

Warden Lawes informed newspapermen covering Sing Sing that he had appointed an executioner, but refused to reveal the name of the man who would be at the controls in the future. Although I virtually rubbed shoulders with reporters and photographers when entering the prison, they did not suspect that I was the one. Perhaps my appearance was not what they had imagined an executioner's would be.

The prison telephoned me to report on Friday night. I went up to Ossining, and about eight o'clock–three hours before the condemned slayer was to have walked "the last mile"–the governor granted a reprieve. Ross never did go to the chair, his sentence finally being commuted to life imprisonment.

Until I threw the switch twice less than a week later, the papers predicted that unusual measures would be taken to conceal the identity of the new executioner. They stated that he would sneak into Sing Sing unobserved, and that he would wear a mask or robe while performing his task. Of course, no such plans were ever contemplated by the warden or me. The stories originated in the fertile brains of reporters, just as have so many other equally false ones about me.

January 28, 1926, when two men died by my hand, was a cold, blustery day. Early that morning, a sixty-mile gale blew into New York from the West, sending the mercury tumbling to twelve degrees above zero by nightfall. The bitterness of the weather increased as I left my home for Sing Sing.

At the prison, I was summoned to the warden's office, then located in his house. It was apparent that he was apprehensive.

"How do you feel?" were his first words. "I'm fine, Warden," I answered.

"That's good." He appeared much relieved.

"I realize, Warden," I said, "that you're worried tonight because this is my first time here. You needn't be, though. I know it's been a good while since I worked with Davis, but I'm sure I won't have any trouble. Everything will be all right."

"I hope so," he replied.

With Chief Engineer Shanahan and George Ogle, "an electrical engineer who assisted the warden in procuring a suitable man for Hulbert's place, I went down to the death chamber about an hour before the execution to make the necessary preparations and test the chair. The two men ticketed for death that night were Luigi Rapito and Emil Klatt. The latter was to pay for a murder he had committed ten years earlier. During the day, Rapito had exhibited so many signs of weakness that it was thought he might have to be carried to his doom. For this reason, he was to go first.

As the fatal hour of eleven approached, I grew uneasy. The death chamber suddenly became intolerably hot and uncomfortable. I began to wish that, if these men must die for their crimes, only one would have to go that night. My responsibility, then, would not be so great. I tried to hide any indications of nervousness by constantly moistening the electrodes. I had decided that I would affix the headpiece on the men.

After the doctors and guards had taken their positions and the witnesses had been seated, Rapito, pale and trembling and mumbling a prayer, was led into the room. I did not look at him as he slipped into the chair. I soon had the head electrode on him, and guards adjusted the leg electrode, the straps, and the mask. Then I walked over to the controls. At a signal from Ogle, I threw the switch.

Except for being fearful of a mishap, I do not recall experiencing any particular emotion while the deadly current streaked through the body in the chair. My principal concern at the moment was that this man die quickly and painlessly. There must be nothing which might cause him any suffering or add to the tension of those present.

Half of my night's work was done when I pulled out the switch at the end of two minutes. So far, there had been no trouble, no unforeseen incident. Rapito's execution had been no different from most of those at Sing Sing. I hoped the next one would be the same.

Klatt was defiant as he entered the death chamber. Standing in front of the chair, he asked permission of Warden Lawes to speak. The warden nodded his consent.

"I hope McNamara will have to stay here until 1940," Klatt declared bitterly. "He did me a great wrong. That is all I have to say." William McNamara, a lifer and an accomplice in the murder, had furnished the information which resulted in Klatt's conviction.

The doomed man seemed in no hurry, and took his time getting seated. He wanted to live as long as the law would allow. In less than three minutes, his body lay alongside Rapito's in the autopsy room, and the witnesses were filing out of the death chamber.

There was no opportunity for me to see Warden Lawes after these executions. However, Dr. Charles C. Sweet, the prison physician, and Ogle assured me that everything had been all right.

My wife was waiting up for me when I got home, but asked no questions. She never does. My son, on the other hand, inquired as to how things had gone. He is usually interested, and I frequently talk over some of my cases with him.

Bob has ridden to four of the prisons with me on several occasions. He has been inside a death chamber, and has seen an electric chair. He has also been in Sing Sing's powerhouse while I was sending a man into eternity. But he has never expressed a desire to witness an electrocution.

Beginning with this double execution, I have kept a careful record of all my cases. A page–sometimes more than one—is devoted to each. There are noted the name of the individual, the nature of his crime, and how he went to his death. This information is set down while the facts are still fresh in my mind. From these accounts, I have been able to reach various conclusions, which I will discuss later.

A week after my first assignment, I was called to Sing Sing again, this time also to electrocute two prisoners. I would not mention this incident had not the first man made a rather strange statement. He was Matthew Wasser, of Buffalo, one of a group of six convicted of a Niagara Falls holdup in which a paymaster was fatally shot. He was the only one of the sextet to be sentenced to death.

Standing beside the electric chair, the doomed man addressed Warden Lawes in a firm voice:

"I want to say I am legally an innocent man going to my death. But I also want to tell you that I earnestly hope you will not be successful in the movement you are undertaking toward abolishing that." He pointed to the chair.

Wasser, who had adopted the surname of his foster parents, had preferred death to life imprisonment He did not believe that life was worth living. Perhaps he had good reason for feeling that way. Years before, his mother had been brutally slain by his father, who was subsequently executed for the crime.

Although prisons with death chairs are equipped with electrodes, Hulbert had always taken his own for use in an emergency or when several people were executed on the same day. I, too, thought this was a wise thing to do. As there were no electrodes on the market, I had to make a set.

"Elephant-ear" sponges (so called because of their large size) were needed, so I sent my son to a New York City store to get them. While the merchant was wrapping them up, he remarked that the last man to whom he had sold sponges of this kind wanted them for an execution.

"Is that right?" Bob said. He did not reveal that he was buying them for the same purpose.

To make the headpiece, I procured an ordinary football helmet from a sporting goods establishment. This I cut to the proper shape, and lined it with the sponges. I also fashioned a leg electrode.

These two electrodes I carried in a small bag. Thus came into being the "little black bag" about which so much has been written. I used my own electrodes now and then for it little more than a year and a half, but finally decided to leave them at home since they were so seldom needed. The last person on whom they were placed was a woman—Ruth Snyder.

Besides New York, Hulbert had served two other states—Massachusetts and New Jersey. Both of these were left without an executioner when he resigned his Sing Sing post, and they soon had to look for one.

A man who had murdered a friend while he slept was scheduled to die in Massachusetts in the spring of 1926. Warden William Hendry of the state prison at Charlestown obtained my name from Warden Lawes, and asked me to meet him in a New York City hotel. Following a short conference, Warden Hendry offered me the Massachusetts job, and I accepted. I executed the man that May fifth.

Nine months passed from the time I was appointed by Warden Lawes until it became public knowledge that I was the executioner. During this period, I had closed the switch on eleven men, ten at Sing Sing. Newspapermen had seen me enter and leave the prisons. They had watched me officiate in the death chambers. Yet they had been unsuccessful in learning my name. Most referred to me in their stories as merely "the new executioner"; a few spoke of me as "Mr. X."

The more we attempted to shroud my identity in mystery, the more determined the reporters were to find out who I was. A New York *World* staff correspondent trailed me home from Sing Sing one night, and discovered the facts. He published a story; but, at the request of

Warden Lawes, failed to disclose my name and address. The Brooklyn *Daily Eagle* did the same, explaining to its readers that it had no desire to embarrass me.

When other newspapers and press services penetrated my wall of privacy, they were not so considerate. The premises were overrun with reporters and photographers. My wife spent most of the day answering the door and the telephone. She met me several blocks from the house as I was returning home late in the afternoon, and told me what had happened. We sat in our automobile for a while in the hope that the newspapermen would leave, but two enterprising reporters managed to find us.

The revelation of my identity "broke" in the papers the next day, a Sunday. Fortunately for me, the state election was only two days away, and the spotlight was turned on the gubernatorial contest between Alfred E. Smith, the incumbent, and Ogden L. Mills. Most of the papers, therefore, did not give the story the space and position which they otherwise might have.

We had expected Gertrude to be disturbed by the news, but she surprised us. At the breakfast table, she read of my prison connection. A rather amused smile came over her face.

"So that's where you've been going these Thursday nights," she said to me.

"Yes, that's right," I admitted.

"Well, the cat's out of the bag now," she said. "Maybe you'll not keep any secrets from me after this."

That was the casual manner in which Gertrude accepted my unusual occupation. She believes, as do the other members of the family, that my work is a necessary one so long as capital punishment exists; that it is better that someone like myself, in whose heart there is no vengeance, carry out the law.

Needless to say, the publicity resulted in considerable annoyance to all of us. Nearly every mail brought "crank" letters—some even threatening my life unless I relinquished the post of executioner. Telephone calls from strangers were so frequent that I had to arrange for an unlisted number to put a stop to them.

After publication of the story, I received a note from Warden Hendry assuring me that the Massachusetts authorities had not given out my name. Sing Sing officials declined to discuss the matter with reporters, and Warden Lawes has never referred to it in any of our conversations. He doubtless realized that I was entirely blameless for what had happened.

It was rumored for a time that the notoriety I received so disturbed me that I intended to give up the work. No such thought entered my mind. In fact, only a month later I performed my first execution for New Jersey at the Trenton penitentiary.

Pennsylvania was next to engage my services. Maurice Broderick, the chief engineer at the Rockview Branch of the Western State Penitentiary in Bellefonte, had also acted as executioner until he was accidentally killed by a falling crane in the summer of 1926. Once when Broderick was ill, a prisoner was to go to the chair, and Warden Stanley P. Ashe had to send for the executioner of a near-by state.

A lock switch is in the death chamber at Bellefonte; that is, it is one which cannot be opened without releasing a button on the handle. The man employed to perform the execution apparently was not familiar with this kind of switch.

Everything ran smoothly until after the final shock. When the executioner was ready to break the circuit, the switch would not budge. He had failed to release the lock. Officials and witnesses stared horrified at the nervous executioner as he struggled vainly to turn off the current. The delay was causing considerable burning of the body in the chair. Finally, an officer who possessed some knowledge of the apparatus stepped over to the control board and pushed the button. The switch then opened.

In selecting another executioner after Broderick's death, the authorities decided that he must be a thoroughly competent electrician, and not be associated with the penitentiary in any way. They communicated with me.

I received three notices from Pennsylvania of a scheduled execution before I put a person to death for that state. The condemned man was reprieved twice, and it was unnecessary for me to go to Bellefonte. On December 27, 1926, my first trip, he and another prisoner went to the chair.

During my first year as an official executioner, eighteen convicted slayers died by electricity controlled by my hand. None of these attracted much attention, except possibly in those localities where the crimes were committed.

Thirty-five executions were performed by me in 1927. It was in this year that I had my first case which evoked world-wide publicity. The date was August 22, and those who paid the supreme penalty were Nicola Sacco, Bartolomeo Vanzetti, and an obscure murderer, Celestino F. Madeiras.

Prior to the Sacco-Vanzetti affair, I saw no need for police protection for my family or myself. True, I had received a number of threatening letters after my name and address were printed; but these did not alarm me. Several friends and prison officials have urged me from time to time to carry a gun, especially when on a mission for the state. However, I have not done so. If anyone is bent on taking my life, I seriously doubt that a weapon on my person would be of much use to me.

About three weeks before the two famous radicals went to the chair, bombs were set off in New York City and elsewhere, presumably in protest against the impending executions. Because I was to put the men to death for the State of Massachusetts, illustrated articles about me appeared in numerous publications. The police read some of these stories, and thought it wise to guard my home. Consequently, I found a patrolman stationed on my property when I returned from New Jersey one night early in August.

The newspapers stated that we had requested the police guard. One added that I sat evenings in a rocking chair with a high-powered rifle, a double-barreled shotgun, and many rounds of ammunition at my side. My wife also was reported on the verge of hysteria. There was, of course, no truth in any of these stories.

A police guard continued until some time after the end of the Sacco-Vanzetti case. Then, at my suggestion, it was removed. Perhaps this was a mistake, for several months following the greatly publicized execution of Ruth Snyder and Henry Judd Gray on January 12, 1928, something of a serious nature occurred that might have been prevented by the presence of a patrolman in front of our house.

A VIOLENT PROTEST

To be blasted almost out of bed in the middle of the night is not the most pleasant thing. Neither does it add to one's peace of mind to know that the act was intentional and deliberate, and that the primary object was one's death. Yet this is what happened to my family and me on May 18, 1928.

There had been nothing to forewarn us of disaster. More than three months had passed since the receipt of the last threatening letter. No suspicious characters had been seen loitering in the vicinity. In fact, everything had been very quiet—perhaps too quiet.

After dinner that mid-May evening, Mrs. Elliott and I drove to the business section of town to buy several pieces of furniture we had wanted for some time. We returned home early, and read for a while. The young people were out, and were not expected until quite late: Little dreaming what was in store for us before the next day dawned, my wife and I retired shortly after 10 o'clock.

Bob and a cousin, Thomas Lang, who was visiting us, came in about midnight. Gertrude followed half an hour later. All had entered by the front door, and would probably have seen any but the smallest object on the porch. By one o'clock, the entire household was abed and asleep.

Ten minutes or so after one, we were suddenly awakened by a loud explosion. My first sensation was as though I were stunned. I felt the compression of air against my eardrums. The house seemed to shiver. There was the wild jangle of crashing window glass and the dull thud of things falling.

Earthquake, I thought first; then, cyclone. But my third and almost instant guess was correct–a bomb!

Mrs. Elliott did not scream. She simply sat up in bed and looked around her. I recall noting that, and, with the queer detachment that comes to one in such an emergency, admiring her for it.

In a few seconds all was still. I jumped out of bed and dashed to the window. What I saw below confirmed my surmise. The house had been bombed.

"Well, Belle, they got us at last," I said to my wife. "I hope the children are all right."

Throwing around us what articles of clothing were nearest, we groped our way to the other rooms. The house was in total darkness, as the electric wires had been disconnected by the blast. The young people had been startled and shaken a bit, but were safe. All of us stumbled down the stairway, which was bulged from the terrific force of the explosion and covered with plaster and broken glass.

Downstairs, two neighbors were frantically banging at the side door, trying to get in. A policeman, who had hurried to the scene from his post at the corner, was attempting to stop them, warning them not to enter because of the danger of falling walls.

"Our neighbors are in there, and we're going to help them if they need it," they told the officer. He did not interfere further.

They soon broke the lock and were in the house. With their assistance, we got outside. Just then a police car stopped with a screech in front of the place. Fortunately, the ambulance which arrived a minute or two later was not needed.

By this time, the neighborhood was seething with fright and excitement. Lights appeared in houses, and people came running from all directions. A cordon of police was thrown around the entire district. Automobiles were stopped and searched.

After recovering somewhat from the shock, we surveyed the damage. The whole front of the sturdy two-story frame building was wrecked, and all the windows in the house were blown out. A section of the roof was hurled thirty feet, landing on a garage. Plaster had fallen in every room except the one occupied by my wife and me. The two boys got it worst, for their room was directly over the front vestibule. As the plaster started to come down, Bob warned Tom to duck, and the two pulled bedclothes over their heads.

We were not the only ones who suffered from the early-morning bombing. Several other homes in the immediate vicinity were showered with flying pieces of timber and glass, and the windows of a few were smashed, too. A man at work loading a milk truck nearly a block away told the police that he was knocked down by the impact. An owl which had been perching in a tree in our yard was found dead on the sidewalk.

Fortunately, no one was more than scratched, but the nervous systems of a good many were shattered. It was a long time before the neighborhood entirely lost the fear of a repetition of that night's experience.

An investigation by the police revealed that the bomb was a time device containing dynamite and steel particles. The only clues were a black-handled penknife found in the debris, and a report that four men in a red touring car had been seen leaving the section immediately following the blast. Although detectives worked on the case for a reasonable period, the culprits were never captured and brought to justice.

When it became evident that nothing more could be done until daybreak, Mrs. Elliott and I had a cup of tea, and returned to bed. Because of fallen plaster in her room, Gertrude was forced to stay with a neighbor. Bob and Tom remained with the crowd, which by then had been augmented by reporters and photographers.

In spite of what had happened, I soon dozed off, and slept soundly. My wife, however, did not close her eyes the rest of the night. She listened to the noise and voices outside, and wondered whether another and more successful attempt would be made on our lives.

The next day the newspapers were full of stories and pictures of the bombing. They exaggerated somewhat when they stated that part of the house was blown from its foundation, and that we had been thrown from our beds. They were incorrect, also, in saying that we were going to move from Richmond Hill, and that I intended to give up the work as executioner. As a matter of fact, I put a man to death in New Jersey less than two weeks later.

Several publications commented editorially on the bombing, and I particularly agreed with the New York paper that said:

The truth that bomb throwers always defeat their own purposes is vividly emphasized in the act of the desperate criminals who tried to assassinate Robert G. Elliott, executioner at Sing Sing.

The bombers succeeded in damaging Elliott's home and in spreading momentary terror throughout the neighborhood. They succeeded also in driving the public to adopt even more rigid measures than before for its own protection. They have convinced the average citizen more completely than ever that capital punishment is the only way to deal with fiends who carry on a warfare involving death and destruction.

Elliott's death would have done nothing to prevent the execution of other condemned persons. This man is a mere cog in the judicial and penal system of New York State. His passing would have found many other men ready and anxious to carry on his grim duties. Electrocutions would have proceeded without a hitch.

The job of executioner is provided for under laws designed to restrain crime. Many earnest people believe these laws to be unjust in many instances, and much constructive good work has been done to bring about substantial changes. Changes will be made only when a majority of citizens are convinced that it is safe to change them. That day is postponed every time a spectacular murder is committed and every time fiendish men set bombs that imperil life and property.

My wife and I suggested that Gertrude stay at home on the day following the bombing, but she insisted on going to school. She was then in high school finishing preparation for the art course she later completed, and did not want to miss a day. Needless to say, she was a little distracted, as any girl of seventeen would naturally be who had undergone such an experience the night before. When the teacher in one class chided her for lack of concentration, tears crept into Gertrude's eyes. The teacher inquired more gently as to what was bothering her, and on hearing the whole story, excused my daughter for the rest of the day. Thereafter, this teacher was one of her most understanding instructors and friends.

During the day, we did what we could to remove the debris and board up the house. While we were thus engaged, something occurred that has given us many a laugh at Bob's expense: Photographers were swarming all over the place, and one of them snapped my son's picture.

"I don't want my picture in the paper," Bob growled at the cameraman.

"O.K., buddy," said the photographer. "If that's the way you feel about it, I'll give it to you."

He held out a plate which Bob believed had just been removed from the camera. Bob thought he had scored one. Imagine his amazement when his face stared back at him from an afternoon edition of that photographer's newspaper!

All of us slept in the house that night. Outside a policeman stood guard. We were afforded this protection for the next five years, a police booth having been built on the premises. Even now an officer is on duty at the house each May Day and when I am about to perform the execution of a well-known figure.

On the day after the bombing, I received an anonymous letter written in an almost illegible scrawl. It was from Paterson, New Jersey, and although dated May 17, was postmarked a day later. It read:

Do not think for a moment that if you have a dozen policemen to save your property or your life, it is immaterial for your kindness which you have shown toward us as mankind human beings. You are a slob like anyone else, so be very careful before your lights are out. You will get yours for not minding your own business.

The signature was "Trustee," but was probably meant to be "Trusty." The chances are that the illiterate writer of that letter was an ex-convict—perhaps a former trusty whose pal had died in the electric chair or was scheduled to go. As I did not connect this threat with the explosion which made a wreck of our house, I have never mentioned it to the police. If the letter had been postmarked as it was dated, then it might have been significant. What happened, I imagine, was that this bitter person, reading in the newspapers of the bombing, dated the letter May 17, either mistakenly or craftily, and mailed it in an attempt to frighten my family and me.

Two months passed before the restoration of the house was complete. The State of New York, by a special appropriation of the legislature, paid for the repairs, and I personally reimbursed the neighbors for the direct damage to their properties.

It has been generally believed that friends or sympathizers of Sacco and Vanzetti were responsible for the wrecking of my home. Yet the bombing took place nine months after these two radicals went to their doom. To me, this seems like a long time for men bent on vengeance to have waited. However, it is obvious that this violent method was employed to protest the fact that I was society's agent of legal death.

Early in the evening of Washington's Birthday in 1929, reporters called at my home with shocking news.

They informed me that Hulbert, my predecessor, had committed suicide that afternoon. He had gone into the darkest corner of the cellar of his home in Auburn, New York, and shot himself twice with a revolver. His body had been found on the floor two hours later by his son.

The newspapermen inquired as to what I knew about Hulbert, and whether I might be able to advance a reason for his act. I declined to comment. As I have stated before, I saw and talked with Hulbert only on those occasions, when I went to Auburn Prison as Davis' assistant. Moreover, I never communicated with him after that time. My refusal to answer questions caused one paper to print the next day that I "was unmoved when told of the suicide."

Various explanations appeared in the press as to why Hulbert died by his own hand. It was said, for instance, that he was haunted by the memory of those whom he had electrocuted. Frankly, I doubt that his previous work had anything to do with it. Prison officials have remarked to me that he at no time displayed any emotional reaction to throwing the switch.

Hulbert had been a melancholy person for a number of years. His despondency increased as ill health overtook him and he faced blindness. Just a few months before his suicide, his wife had died. These things probably accounted for the fact that he no longer wished to live.

Following Hulbert's death, the equipment he had carried with him when on a grim mission for the state was sent to New Jersey authorities by his relatives. However, I have never used it, preferring that which was more modern.

Because my predecessor took his own life, it has been freely predicted that I would do the same. Part of the caption under a picture of me in a national magazine read that "Elliott ended by hanging himself." That was the most serious misstatement ever published about me. Ordinarily I ignore false reports, but I could not refrain this time from protesting to the editor. Prominent space in the periodical was given to a correction and an apology shortly afterward.

Although Vermont is one of the states I serve, only once have I been called there—a record indicating either that the Green Mountain State is fortunate in the type of its citizens, or that the threat of capital punishment is an effective deterrent.

In the spring of 1932, I received a letter from Warden J. W. McDermott, of the Vermont State Prison at Windsor, stating that he had a prisoner under sentence of death, but no one to carry out the order of the court. Not for thirteen years had Vermont's electric chair been used, he wrote, and no member of the prison staff, from the warden down, had had any experience in the sorry business of putting a man to death. I consented to officiate.

Several days before the execution, which was set for 11:40 P.M. on July 7, I drove to Windsor to inspect and test the apparatus. Both the chair and electrical equipment were in good condition. As the penitentiary had neither electrodes nor a mask, I borrowed the former from the New Jersey State Prison and the latter from Sing Sing.

So that the guards who were to strap the man in the chair would be entirely familiar with their duties, I let them practice on me during the day of the execution. At first, they were a nervous lot; but after they had gone through the procedure several times, they were more composed. However, I decided that, under the circumstances, I had better apply both electrodes and the mask.

Warden McDermott and I dined together that night. During our conversation a little later, the fact was mentioned that while the condemned man knew he had only a few more hours of life, he had not been officially notified.

"I suppose I should go through the formality of telling him that he is to go tonight," said the prison head.

"That is customary, Warden," I said. "After all, he has a right to be told officially."

The warden left to read the death warrant to the doomed man. When he returned, the expression on his face indicated that he had found this an ordeal.

Not long before the execution, the chaplain sought me out. He wanted my permission to talk to the man after he was in the chair. I suggested that he speak to the warden, which he told me he had already done. The warden, he said, preferred to leave the decision to me. I had no objection, and granted his request.

Vermont has no death house, and keeps the people to be executed in a cell in the prison hospital. This building is located some distance from the room in which the chair is set up, which means that the condemned have quite a walk. The prisoner that night trod the longest "last mile" in all my experience.

As soon as the murderer had sat in the chair, the chaplain talked to him. Finally, he asked if he were guilty of the crime of which he had been convicted.

"I trust in God," replied the man on the threshold of eternity. "He knows I am innocent." The clergyman stepped back, a signal to me that he had finished. I threw the switch.

From the moment the prisoner had entered the room until he received the first electric shock, more time had elapsed than in the case of any other person I have executed. This was due to the fact that I applied both electrodes and the mask, and inspected the straps to make sure that they had been properly adjusted. The chaplain, of course, had taken up a minute or two.

Only once have I had anything to do with the installation of an electric chair, and that was in an advisory capacity. When Connecticut substituted electrocution for hanging several years ago, Warden Ralph H. Walker, of the state prison at Wethersfield, telephoned me for an estimate of what a plant and equipment would cost. I gave him an approximate figure and the name of Frederick J. Carr, an electrical engineer and contractor, of Trenton, New Jersey, who had installed such an apparatus for several states and the Philippine Islands.

Carr was chosen to build Connecticut's plant. He agreed, among other things, to be present at the first electrocution, and to guarantee the apparatus if I were the one who operated it. Thus was Connecticut added to the list of states for which I act as executioner.

The chair was installed in the summer of 1936, in. the same chamber where the state had hanged Gerald Chapman and other less notorious murderers. I visited the prison while the work was going on, and inspected the plant after it was completed.

Connecticut's first legal electrocution came sooner than Carr and, I had expected. Carr's wife was in ill health, and he had planned to take her to Florida for two months. Shortly before they were to leave, we learned that a man was scheduled to go to the chair on February 10, 1937. Consequently, unless the prison authorities would not require Carr's presence at the execution, his trip would have to be postponed. The two of us discussed the situation with Warden Walker, and he did not insist on Carr's attendance after I assured him that it would be unnecessary.

Carr's son accompanied me to Wethersfield on the day that the state inaugurated the use of its death chair. Except for two officials who had witnessed an execution at Sing Sing, none at the prison had previously participated in an electrocution. I instructed the officers in the details of the procedure, and we carefully rehearsed every step.

This execution was carried out without difficulty. The only thing unusual was a question raised by the deputy warden. The condemned man had false teeth, and I was asked whether they should be taken out before he started on his walk to the death chamber. As I saw no need for it, they were not removed.

Since I have been official executioner for six Eastern states, all sorts of ridiculous and strange stories have been circulated as to why I became engaged in the work. Perhaps the most fanciful tale of all was brought to my attention not long ago by a newspaperman with whom I have been friendly for years. It seems that a mail carrier in a suburb of Pittsburgh, who asserted that he knew me personally, was telling people that my wife and two of my children had been murdered some years ago. This had made me sour on the world, the postman alleged, and I had taken to the bleak business so I could avenge their deaths.

"I certainly lost no time in driving a nail into that story," the newspaperman wrote me. I am glad that he did, for the deepest conviction I have concerning capital punishment is that vengeance should play no part in it.

DEATH BY LAW

A society that demands the death penalty for murder and other major crimes should know just how the legal killing of a human being is accomplished. It should know, also, exactly what the man whose hand controls the lethal current does when he is acting for the state. These things I propose to tell.

The taking of a life, legally or illegally, is a grim business. Legally, it must be undertaken and carried through as efficiently and humanely as possible. Details must not be slighted, mistakes must be avoided. That is my responsibility.

My first obligation, of course, is always to be on call. Never do I leave my home for any appreciable length of time without informing all of the prison authorities concerned, or ascertaining whether an execution is scheduled for the near future.

As a rule, the death sentence provides that the condemned be electrocuted in a certain week—the exact day and hour being left to the discretion of the warden in charge of the arrangements. Most wardens have set a time which they believe is the most satisfactory. For instance, New York State has its executions on Thursday at eleven P.M., and Pennsylvania on Monday at 12:30 A.M. The latter's former early-morning hour of seven o'clock was changed in May, 1934, because it was

88

considered hard on the doomed prisoner and inconvenient for those who must participate officially in the execution.

Some wardens communicate with me before definitely fixing a date. This is so that my services will not be required at two different places on the same night. Once such a situation arose, and one of the states had to postpone its execution twenty-four hours.

Word that I am to report at a prison comes by letter or telegram well in advance of an execution. The laconic notification I receive from Sing Sing is typical, and reads as follows:

Dear Sir:

This is to inform you that one execution is scheduled for Thursday night, (*Date*), in the case of (*Name and Number*), and we shall expect you to be present at the regular time.

Kindly acknowledge by wire the receipt of this notice.

Very truly yours,

LEWIS E. LAWES

Warden.

Thus begins for me a period of thought and preparation. Plans must be made to insure my punctual arrival at the prison. In New Jersey, I am supposed to be in the prison four hours before the appointed time; in the other five states, approximately two hours. Only once have I been late. That was in Massachusetts, and I was delayed when a New England snowstorm halted railroad traffic. I telegraphed the warden, and he put off the execution until the next night.

Today, I carry no equipment with me to the prisons, and travel either by train or automobile. If I go by car, some member of the family or a friend rides along. I always like company, for I enjoy talking while I drive. When I go to Sing Sing, whoever accompanies me usually waits in the visitors' room or outside the prison until my work is done.

Although many people believe that my failure to appear would prevent the law from running its full course, there has never been an attempt to stop me from reaching my destination. The nearest anyone has come to it was to send me a warning that I would meet a terrible fate on the way.

Upon arriving at Ossining or Trenton, I proceed directly to the prison. In the other cities, I register at a hotel, and call the warden's office. From then until I am needed in the death chamber, I attend a movie, read, or drop around to the prison to check the equipment. At Bellefonte, friends sometimes come up to my room for a chat.

Newspapermen frequently lie in wait for me at the prison, determined to obtain a photograph or some sort of statement. I try to dodge them, and am usually successful. On the occasion of a highly publicized case, a mystified reporter asked the warden: "How on earth did Elliott get in without being seen? We've watched for him all day." The warden dismissed the question with, "Oh, he dropped in the yard in an airplane." What had actually happened was that I entered by a gate at which no newspaperman kept vigil.

Before going to the death chamber, I generally talk with prison officials. Sometimes I am told that the condemned has received a reprieve, or that his sentence has been commuted to life imprisonment. I am always glad to hear these things, for a person should not have to give up his life if there is the slightest doubt as to his guilt. It is far better that a guilty man be spared than that an innocent one die.

No person in my experience has had his execution halted after being brought into the death chamber. A few, however, have been reprieved virtually in the shadow of the chair. Several minutes before he was to have died at Sing Sing, Joseph Bauman, convicted of killing a man in the course of a robbery, was given a short lease on life. Again, twenty-five minutes before he was to have marched to his doom, he was saved by a sixty-day stay. Bauman never went to the chair.

On another night, at Sing Sing, two Bronx gangsters actually received a respite twelve minutes after the time for their executions had passed. The men, Frank

Giordano and Dominick Odierno, had slain a beer runner, and they were to be electrocuted on June 30, 1932. The witnesses had gathered. With everything ready, I waited in the death chamber.

A scant half hour before the scheduled time, Giordano made a desperate attempt to stave off the chair. He said that he had information bearing on the shooting of a five-year-old boy in New York City in 1931. The fatal bullet, he alleged, had been fired by Vincent Coll, notorious gangster, in a running street fight of mobsters. The child had simply been an innocent target. Giordano insisted that he knew what he was talking about, for he had driven the death car. Coll, incidentally, had been "rubbed out" by his enemies early in 1932, when they surprised him in a telephone booth on New York's West Side.

Giordano's statement was 'immediately telephoned to Governor Franklin D. Roosevelt in Albany. The governor, at that moment, was listening to a radio report of the Democratic National Convention in Chicago, which was nominating him for the Presidency of the United States. He asked Warden Lawes to postpone the executions until he called back.

At 11:12 o'clock, the governor ordered a twenty-four-hour reprieve for the two murderers. But they gained little by this respite. On the following day, Giordano retracted what he had said, and the men were put to death that night.

Executions have been delayed on several occasions and for different reasons. George Yarrow, a bus driver who had slain a young girl, was slated to die at the New Jersey State Prison at eight P.M. on June 1, 1928. Shortly before the appointed time, his attorney begged the principal keeper to hold up the proceedings for an hour so he would have an opportunity to get in touch with the governor. The prison official was willing. However, the governor refused to intervene, and Yarrow was executed at 9:08 o'clock.

Fate played macabre tricks on Quincey Wallandz, doomed Cuban who killed his estranged wife in Philadelphia. While the murderer was en route to Rockview Penitentiary to pay the supreme penalty, Governor Gifford Pinchot granted a reprieve on the word of physicians that the condemned man would die of tuberculosis and heart disease within thirty days. But life was stubborn, and the doctors were wrong. Wallandz was still alive at the end of the month. The governor refused any further respites. However, on the morning of the execution, the elements conspired to give the prisoner three more hours of life. A sweeping blizzard disrupted the power for the electrocution, and the prison physician, whose presence was required by law, was snowed in at his home two miles away. Following restoration of the power lines, a sleigh was sent for the doctor.

Another time, a show given by convicts resulted in the postponement of a double execution. Charles Markowitz and Joseph Brown had been found guilty of murdering a police sergeant in a New York cafe hold-up, and were to die in Sing Sing's chair on December 8, 1932. It so happened that this was one of the nights on which the prison's annual revue was to be presented. The incongruity of the two events prompted Warden Lawes to move the time of the execution from Thursday night to 12:30 A.M. Saturday, and the sentence of the court was carried out immediately following the final performance of the revue.

I was instrumental in prolonging the lives of two men in 1939. After I had sent a murderer into eternity at the Massachusetts State Prison one night, I called attention to the fact that the apparatus was obsolete and should be replaced. Later, I wrote the chief electrician about it. My letter was read to a committee of the legislature, which subsequently authorized modernization of the plant. Before this could be done, two youths, Wallace Green and Walter St. Sauveur, who had slain a grocer in a $3.50 robbery, were ordered put to death. They were given a three-month respite while the work was going on.

If a request is to be made of me in connection with an execution, it is usually asked before I go to the death chamber. On the night that Nathan Desatnick died in Massachusetts for drowning his infant daughter, the rabbi urged me to keep my hat on during the execution. I complied with his wish, as did all the others in the chamber.

One of the spiritual advisers of Raymond George, a man who had murdered a Jersey City policeman, came to me on the evening that the condemned prisoner was to expiate his crime. "Please do your best not to mark him on the face, Mr. Elliott," the clergyman pleaded. In spite of the high voltage, I succeeded in fulfilling his request.

Ordinarily, I am the first person to reach the death chamber on an execution night, although members of the prison staff frequently accompany me. Many times I have been the one to open Sing Sing's execution room and snap on the lights. At Rockview Penitentiary; before going to the chamber, I must sign a register. This is required of every person, except prison employees, who is permitted on the floors where the condemned cells and execution and autopsy rooms are located.

Electrocution chambers in most Eastern states are very similar. The death house at Sing Sing is a separate structure. Rockview Penitentiary's occupies a building with the hospital, the place of execution being on the second floor. Some penal institutions have it a part of or connected with another building.

Large enough to accommodate all who must be present when the state settles its account with condemned criminals, the death chamber has a clean-looking appearance. Bright lights illuminate it so that everything which occurs can be clearly seen. The only furnishings are the electric chair and seats for the witnesses.

Built of heavy wood, probably by convicts in the prison carpenter shop, the electric chair is bolted to the floor, and is surrounded by a rubber mat. Its tilted back is high, its arms broad. An adjustable rubber-padded headrest, normally left in a vertical position, is attached to the back. The chair is supported by three legs—two behind and a broad one in front. To the latter are fastened the ankle grips. Eight strong leather straps dangle from points where they will most firmly bind the chest, abdomen, each upper arm, each wrist, and each ankle.

Wires in pipes under the floor carry the current. One leads to the front of the chair, the other to the top. On the lower wire is fitted the leg electrode; on the upper, the headpiece, or helmet. The electrodes are faced with sponge, through which the current passes into the body.

Not far from the chair are the controls. At Trenton, the instrument panel is immediately behind the death seat—so close, in fact, that I could stand by the switch and reach out and touch the dying figure. Sing Sing's switchboard is located in an alcove. Those of the other prisons are in, plain view, a few feet to one side of the chair.

Alternating current is used, and is produced by a special generator within the prison or obtained from the outside power system. Regulators vary the voltage up to 2,200. In nearly all of the prisons, this is accomplished with a transformer equipped with a movable core. I generally apply not more than 2,000 volts. As the current for the chair is on a separate circuit, the prison lights, contrary to popular belief, do not dim when the death-chamber switch is thrown.

The average number of amperes in an electrocution is eleven. The amperage (or amount of current) is governed by the resistance of the body. In other words, if the resistance of the body is low, a greater quantity of electricity flows through it. I have had cases in which the resistance was so high that the number of amperes was only seven, and again when it was so low that the body took sixteen.

Curiously enough, physical size and apparent strength seem to have no influence on the amperage. The resistance of an individual to a shock of electricity can change from day to day, according to conditions of temperature and moisture. A man or a woman afflicted with tuberculosis can resist the blow of high voltage more than someone in normal health. The presence of less chloride in the blood of such a person is probably the reason for this.

My first task on arriving in the death chamber is to check the equipment which human ingenuity has fashioned with infinite skill to destroy life. Electricians have gone over the generators during the day to be sure that they operate properly, but there are many other things which must be inspected. Although what goes on in the execution room is not likely to be heard outside, I work as quietly as possible. I would not want any sound of the preparations to reach the person or persons who must die that night. The slightest noise would cause those last torturous minutes to be even mare unbearable.

Only once have I heard any commotion in the death cells. That was at Trenton when a prisoner started to walk his "last mile." The other inmates of death raw yelled and pounded on the bars. They cursed me and everybody else associated with the state's legal killings, and kept up their protest against capital punishment until quieted by the guards. Their demonstration not only added to the tension in the execution room, but also increased the nervousness of the man on the threshold of eternity.

I might say here that I do not wear in the death chamber any special "working" clothes, as one newspaper writer described my attire. Neither are my hands covered with rubber gloves, far I see no need far it.

In examining the chair, I make certain that it is hooked up and that no wires are broken, I inspect the adjusting screws, test the strength of the straps, and determine whether the buckles work freely. A strap did break during an execution, and I try to prevent a repetition of this.

Then I look to see if the mask is where it should be, and ascertain whether its strap and buckle are sound, The mask, usually a black leather band with an .opening far the nostrils and mouth, serves a double purpose: that of shielding the face and holding the head in place against

95

the headrest. At Rockview Penitentiary, the mask covers the entire face.

A pail of brine—nothing more than a solution of common salt and water—is prepared. In this are soaked the sponges of the electrodes to insure a good contact. One night I found that the supply of salt was exhausted, and we had to hurry out and get some.

My next step is to test the apparatus. This is accomplished in either of two ways. One is to attach a board of electric lights to the wires leading to the chair, and illumination of the bulbs furnishes evidence that current is passing through. The other is to put the two electrodes in a bucket of water, with perhaps a pinch of salt, and close the circuit. If the water heats up, I know that electricity is flowing.

Certain information about the condemned is necessary if I am to guard against mishaps. I must know his general physical specifications, such as his size and height. These facts I obtain from the guards or the doctors, as I never see the prisoner until he enters the death chamber.

The chair will accommodate people of all sizes, but extremely tall or short persons require special preparation. The tallest I can recall was Richard C. Bach, twenty-five years old, who was executed in Pennsylvania in 1934. He was a powerful physical specimen, six feet, seven inches in height. It was with difficulty that we strapped the mask to the top of the chair that morning. I suggested to the deputy warden that he hold the strap in place, but he did not take kindly to the idea. I could hardly blame him.

During one man's imprisonment, his leg had become very small at the calf, and there was danger that, unless something were done, the electrode would slip. To insure its remaining snug, I inserted three thicknesses of sponge.

For the regulation of the head electrode, I find out the size of the hat worn by the doomed prisoner. I also inquire whether his hair has been cut short in the back. I did not make it a point to ask about this until after an experience in Massachusetts in 1935. On that occasion, three young men—Murton and Irving Millen and Abraham Faber—were brought to the chair, and, for some reason, had not had their hair clipped. All had bushy, oily hair, especially Irving. As a consequence, the head electrode could not come in contact with the flesh, thus burning the hair and causing considerable smoke.

Some cases present problems or give rise to questions. A doctor told me one night at Rockview Penitentiary that the condemned man's heart was on the wrong side, and he wondered whether this would complicate matters. I assured him that it would not. Another murderer had swallowed parts of a bed spring in an attempted suicide, and they had not been removed. Except for a second application of the current before he was pronounced dead, his execution was like most others. Then there was the aged killer of a little girl in New York who had stuck pins and needles in his body because he enjoyed the sensation. Speculation was rife as to what might happen when the current coursed through him. Some expected to see sparks fly in all directions, but nothing unusual happened.

In three of the states where I preside over the lethal switch—New York, New Jersey, and Connecticut—the lower electrode is attached to the calf of the right leg. For no particular reason that I know, it is the left leg in Pennsylvania, Massachusetts, and Vermont. However, three times we have had no choice. In each instance, the man to be put to death had only one leg.

It is always of primary concern to me to learn how the condemned is bearing up, and whether he has embraced a religious faith. I get this information from the prison chaplain or an officer who has been with the prisoner much of the day. The fact that the person who is to be executed has made his peace with his Maker is as much comfort to me as to his spiritual adviser. I have seen how a belief in religion and the hereafter strengthens a man, even the most hardened, in the waning hours of his life.

97

When more than one person is ticketed for death on the same night, the order of their going is determined in advance. The weakest—that is, the one least able to stand up under the ordeal of waiting his turn is first. The others follow according to their physical and mental condition.

About twenty minutes or so before execution time, the doctors and the officers whose duty it is to strap the condemned in the chair enter the death chamber.

They stand around in little groups, talking in low voices. The principal keeper or deputy warden, as the case may be, arrives a few minutes later to check on all arrangements for this elaborately planned ceremony of death. He asks me if everything is ready. I reply that it is.

I carry the electrodes to the chair, and try the wires in the binding posts. I make sure that the thumb screws are tight enough to hold the "lead-in" wires in place. Then I soak the electrodes in the saline solution, squeezing out the sponges to leave the condition of moisture which experience has taught me is right. Should the sponges be too wet and drip, sparks may follow the water. On the other hand, if they are dry, sparking will result.

After this, I go to the switchboard. The indicator on the voltmeter is pointing to 2,000. Time is getting shorter. The physician and officers take their positions. Witnesses file into the room. The time has come.

If in a state where testing the chair in front of the witnesses is required, I now do so with a board of lights. In Pennsylvania, when the bulbs are illuminated, the prison physician announces, "The lights show that there are 2,000 volts passing through the chair." The test completed, I take the leg electrode to the chair, and place the "lead-in" wire in the binding post. The electrode is ready for the guard who affixes it.

The principal keeper or deputy warden looks at me inquiringly. I nod. He leaves the room to bring in the man or woman to be executed. While he is gone, I continue to moisten the head electrode. I do this to be busy during the short wait and to keep the sponge from drying out. A warden once remarked that watching me at this time made him very nervous.

In a minute, there is a soft rap on the door. A guard opens it. The prison official enters, followed by the clergyman (if the condemned person has not refused the services of one), the prisoner, and a guard or two. I step to the rear of the chair, the head electrode in my hand. The condemned comes directly to the death seat.

Should he have anything to say, he usually does so now. In all prisons except Rockview Penitentiary, death-chamber statements are permitted. But even at Rockview, a condemned person occasionally talks. The principal keeper of the New Jersey State Prison sometimes invites the prisoner to speak.

When it appears that the person to die wants to say something, I wait for him. Once, at Trenton, as I was putting the mask over a killer's face, he seemed about to speak. I stopped what I was doing, and stepped aside. But he remained silent, and I finished strapping his head in place.

It has been stated that I object to speeches in the execution room. That is not true. But I do believe that talking at length should be prohibited. Except possibly for providing good newspaper copy, this serves only to add to the tenseness of the situation, and often causes the condemned to become hysterical and difficult to handle.

As soon as the prisoner is seated in the chair, the guards spring into action. Pushing up the slit trouser leg, one applies the lower electrode. (If the prisoner is a woman, the stocking has already been rolled down to the ankle.) Other officers handle the straps.

I always affix the head electrode, which is attached to the base of the skull and is held secure by a strap under the chin. Occasionally, a condemned person leans forward to watch the straps being adjusted on his legs, and I have to gently pull his head back. At several prisons, with the help of an officer, I put the mask in place. I was startled one morning when a man sitting in Pennsylvania's electric chair addressed me as I was about to cover his face. "Leave that off," he said, meaning the mask. I could not grant his wish.

About a minute passes from the instant the condemned enters the death chamber until he is fully strapped in the chair and the electrodes and mask are adjusted. If the prisoner speaks, the time, of course, is longer. I do my work deliberately and carefully, hurrying only when I see that the person to be executed is particularly nervous or apparently on the verge of collapse.

A final quick inspection of the electrodes and straps, and I step to the instrument board. The switch in four of the prisons opens in oil so that there will be no sparking. At every prison except one, it is so constructed as to be thrown upward. This is a precaution against the possibility of its falling and dosing the circuit prematurely. In New Jersey and Connecticut, I spin a wheel after throwing the switch, and regulate the voltage with it.

When I first became official executioner, a signal was given to turn on the electricity. The chief physician did this, the object being to have the current applied at the moment the lungs were empty. Thus it was hoped to avoid the loud, gurgling noise that follows when the current strikes the body while the lungs are full of air. The practice has been generally abandoned because the doctors at times found it impossible to see the movements of the condemned's chest. Now, only at the New Jersey State Prison is there a signal. At all other places, I throw the switch at what I believe to be the most opportune and humane instant.

I have often wondered what goes on in the mind of the person about to be hurled into the next world as, trussed and blindfolded, he awaits the bolt of lightning that travels in wires. Do the events of his wasted life parade before him in rapid succession? Does terror beyond our comprehension seize him? Or does some sort of peace descend upon him, easing those last moments? These things we will never know.

Before sending the lethal current on its journey of destruction, I glance again at the chair. I want to be sure that no one is too near it. Then I throw the switch. As I do so, I often pray silently, "May God have mercy on your soul."

The figure in the chair pitches forward, straining against the straps. There is the whining cry of the current, and a crackling, sizzling sound. The body turns a vivid red. Sparks often shoot from the electrodes. A wisp of white or dull gray smoke may rise from the top of the head or the leg on which the electrode is attached. This is produced by the drying out of the sponge, singed hair, and, despite every effort to prevent it, sometimes burning flesh. An offensive odor is generally present.

Many people are of the impression that I cannot see the chair while the current is on. As a matter of fact, I keep my eyes on it almost constantly. For the safety of those who must be near it, I would not perform an execution unless I were able to see the chair all the time. If, for any reason, someone should get too close, I would want to know immediately so I could shut off the current. Moreover, there is always the possibility of a mishap, and this necessitates my watching what is going on.

At one time, the executioner and his switch were located in a separate room. In the early days at Dannemora, when Davis was New York State's agent of death, a man was stationed at a concealed switch, with Davis at another in full view of the witnesses. The executioner threw his switch, then signaled to his colleague, who closed the circuit. Davis regulated the current, and turned it off when he thought it had accomplished its purpose. Thus, probably, the belief that I am out of sight.

Five seconds after the initial shock of 2,000 volts, I decrease the current to 1,000 volts or somewhat under. The purpose of this is to avoid sparking and needless burning. At the end of half a minute, I increase it to 1,800 or 2,000 volts, and after another few seconds, cut it down again. This is repeated at half-minute intervals. As the current is increased and lowered, the body in the chair rises and sinks. Finally, after the fifth shock, I reduce the current gradually.

Lowering the current slowly following the final shock is my own idea. I believe that it effectively weakens the heart and stops the action. Perhaps this is a fallacy, but once or twice when I have not done it, the heart has continued to beat after the current was turned off.

I time the process by a wrist watch, a gift from my wife. It is like those used by nurses, being especially equipped with a large second hand. At two of the prisons, an officer acts as timekeeper. Standing near by, he tells me how long a certain voltage has been on and the exact instant the amount should be raised or lowered. In Sing Sing, he also switches on a ventilating fan after an execution to free the room of any smoke or odor.

A study of how the heart and muscles react to electricity was made on two occasions in my experience. One night, George Ogle, of whom I have spoken before, obtained Warden Lawes' permission to feel a man while current tore through him. Standing by the chair and wearing rubber gloves, Ogle ran his hands over the straining body. He noted the muscular contraction and the beat of the heart. On another night at Sing Sing, an electrocardiograph was attached to the condemned prisoner to record the heart action.

When I first officiated as executioner, the current was arbitrarily shut off at the end of two minutes. As a result, doctors often found the heart still beating, and the electricity had to be applied again. To prevent this, on several subsequent occasions, I kept the switch closed for three full minutes. Each time the body was badly burned, so two and a half minutes was decided upon. But even this proved a little too long. One night at Sing Sing, the prison physician suggested that I try a minute and a half. I did, and he had to call for the current again. Now, I leave it on for slightly more than two minutes, and rarely is a second application necessary.

After the electricity is turned off, the condemned person's chest is bared, and the perspiration wiped away with a towel. I do this in all of the prisons, except Sing Sing. One or more doctors step to the chair, and listen with a stethoscope for the beat of the heart. If satisfied that all life is extinct, the prison physician declares, "I pronounce this man [or woman] dead."

I recall an instance when the only doctor in the death chamber was attending his first execution. Shortly after I arrived, he sought me out, and wanted to know exactly what his duties were to be. I explained. "Suppose the man isn't dead?" he asked. I assured him that there was very little likelihood of such being the case. When the time came for him to examine the body in the chair, the doctor was visibly nervous, but managed to do what was expected of him.

As soon as the prisoner is pronounced dead, the limp body is unstrapped, lifted onto a hospital stretcher with rubber wheels, and trundled into another room. There, if required by law, as is the case in most states, an autopsy is performed. Sometimes I examine the body to see whether it has been burned.

Upon finishing my work, I leave the prison. I feel as though a great burden has been lifted from me, for I never permit myself to relax for a second during an execution. If I am at either Ossining or Trenton, I return home immediately. In the other cities, I spend the rest of the night at a hotel, departing for Richmond Hill early the next day.

Often I have been asked whether the condemned suffers any pain when struck by man-made lightning. All scientific and practical evidence points to the fact that death by electricity is painless and certain. The first terrific shock of 2,000 volts shatters the person's nervous system instantaneously and beyond recall, and paralyzes the brain before the nerves can register any pain. Medical experts declare that unconsciousness is produced in less than one two-hundred and fortieth of a second. This, then, is as humane as ordered death can possibly be.

At one execution I performed, the condemned man, in a spirit of bravado with which he tried to hide his fear, said as he was being strapped in the chair: "Doc, my last act is going to be for science. We'll see how fast this juice really works. The moment I feel it, I'll wiggle a finger." He did not wiggle his finger.

The heat which the electricity produces in the electrodes and in the body is almost unbelievable. There was a night in my experience when the copper in the leg electrode was actually melted. The average body temperature after the current has been on for two minutes is one hundred and thirty-eight degrees.

As an instrument of death, today's electric chair is efficient and quick. I would suggest only two improvements. One is that an electrode be placed over the prisoner's heart, thus stopping the action of this vital organ almost as soon as the electricity is applied. The other is the employment of clamps instead of straps to hold the person in the chair. This would expedite the process of preparing the condemned for the current, and the resulting reduction of a few seconds would make the method even more humane. Where clamps are used in prisons, they have been found practical.

There is one important thing that should be done in every state I serve as executioner. I should have a regular assistant–a man who would help me at all executions and would be trained in the work. He could substitute for me in the event that, for some reason, I should be unable to report, and would be my logical successor when I resign.

The need for an assistant executioner has been demonstrated several times. It was shown in 1939, when, due to illness, I could not officiate at a few electrocutions. Up to then, I had been present whenever my services were required. Had I had an assistant, he could have taken my place while I was incapacitated, and the wardens would have been spared the trouble of procuring a substitute, probably someone who had never before acted in such a capacity.

On one occasion, shortly after I started in the work, I urged a warden to give me a helper. He saw no necessity for it in view of the fact that an electrician besides me then attended all executions performed at that prison. I have not broached the subject to the heads of the other prisons. But I do believe that some arrangements should be made for an assistant. I would fee1 better, the wardens would have less to worry about with in connection with executions, and the states would be sure of a capable man to carry on after I have relinquished the post.

THEIR "LAST MILE"

The ability to meet an emergency which the human mind possesses has always been a marvel to me. Particularly true is this in the case of the person who walks "the last mile" to the electric chair, knowing full well that certain death awaits him there.

Though he may succeed in hiding his emotions from the world, as so many do, I am convinced that fear grips his heart. It may be the mystery of what lies beyond the grave or the thought that he might suffer intense pain as life departs which terrorizes him.

Yet, in spite of extreme fear, a remarkably high percentage of those whom I have executed have borne up well during their last moments on earth. They have gone to their deaths courageously and outwardly calm. The sustaining force has been bravado, pride, defiance, hate, or even a weary acquiescence. Religious belief, too, has played a vital part in enabling many to meet their fate stoically.

Of course, it has been necessary to assist some to the chair. A few have been brought into the death chamber in such a dazed condition that they appeared oblivious to their surroundings. Several have screamed hysterically or begged for mercy until the lethal current silenced them. But in all my prison experience, only one had to be carried in.

106

The ages of those I have sent into eternity have varied. The youngest was eighteen, the oldest seventy. Nearly early three-fourths have been under thirty. Only about eight per cent have been over forty.

What the condemned do and how they act while awaiting death I know from information given me by prison officials, physicians, and clergymen with whom I have talked. Some are model prisoners; others are troublesome from the very day they enter the death cells. There are those who, when not bemoaning their plight, complain about everything. Occasionally, one attempts suicide; but, due to precautionary measures, only rarely are such efforts successful.

A long time elapses before most of them pay their debt to society. They spend months of torment while their appeals are being studied and other moves made to save them. Sacco and Vanzetti furnish a notable example of this. Six years passed between their conviction and the night they went to the chair. But there have been exceptions to the rule. In Pennsylvania, I executed Harry Coon, slayer of a little girl, sixty-five days after he was found guilty, and William Watkins, friendless killer of a farmer, seventy-seven days following sentence.

Doomed prisoners spend their hours in reading, writing letters, playing checkers, and the like. Paul Jaworski, notorious Pittsburgh bandit leader and confessed killer of seven men, became engrossed in a continued magazine story. When he learned that he would have to die before finishing the serial, he said, "Gee, it's tough not to know how this thing ends." The publisher heard about it, and sent him an advance copy of the final installment.

I have been told that inmates of the death house speak of me now and then. Once a prisoner in New Jersey inquired as to what kind of man I was and whether I knew my business. The guard assured him that I was an expert electrician. "That's good," the murderer commented. "I just want to be sure that the job will be done right." In the death chamber, he asked that I be pointed out to him. He looked at me for a few seconds, and, apparently satisfied, nodded and sat down in the chair.

It always seems ironical to me when science is called upon to save a human life so it can be taken a short time later by the state. This has happened a number of times. Men and women have been operated on or treated for other ailments in order that they would not "cheat the chair," as the newspapers term it. Executions have been postponed because the condemned were ill. Prisoners who have gone temporarily insane while in the death house have been reprieved until their sanity was restored.

There are times when condemned persons have refused surgical or medical aid. Ross Caccamise, slayer of a cigar merchant, was one of these. He was stricken with appendicitis in the death house six months before he was scheduled to die. Physicians urged an operation, but he would not consent. Despite this, however, he recovered sufficiently to stumble to the chair.

William (Two-Gun) Turner might still be alive had he been co-operative. On the day originally set for his execution, he received a two weeks' reprieve so that doctors could thoroughly test his sanity. As part of the examination, they wanted to tap his spine for a specimen of fluid, but he would not permit it.

The highly imaginative probably suffer more intensely than the others. They die not once, but a score of times. In one state I serve, a poor wretch awaiting his turn pleaded with the warden to let him see the chair. He said he had a horrible mental picture of it that was driving him mad, and believed that if he could examine the apparatus, he would be less afraid. With misgivings, the warden finally granted the unusual request. The prisoner inspected the chair, and seemed strangely relieved afterward.

A youth of twenty who was to be executed with two his pals, was to lead the death march because it was thought that he was the weakest. When he learned of this, he sent for the warden.

"I want to die game," he said pitifully, "but I know I won't if I have to go first. If the others went ahead me, I'm sure I'd be all right. It would give me courage."

The warden understood, and changed the order. The youth was the third to go. Although visibly nervous, he managed to conceal the terror that had hold of him.

Another doomed man made a similar request—but not for the same reason. On the day of his execution, he asked the warden to have his companions in crime precede him to the chair so that he could watch them walk "the last mile." "That's something I've always had a hankering to see," he explained. His request was granted.

To the very end, all condemned men and women cling to the hope that they will be spared by getting a new trial, a reprieve, or a commutation of sentence. Joseph Senna, a lonesome murderer who had had no visitors while in Sing Sing's death house, expressed this when he said to his keepers: "I have no friends, but still I hope for a reprieve. I guess everybody does." There was no stay for him; but, as in the cases of so many others, the possibility that there might be one helped to buoy him up during those last days.

A few make desperate last-minute efforts to escape the supreme penalty by trying to bargain with the authorities. In exchange for their lives or a respite from death, they promise to uncover further details of the murder or to involve others, or agree to furnish in-formation concerning unsolved crimes. At times, if it is believed that the men are telling the truth, their bids are accepted, and the prisoners become witnesses for the state.

When everything else fails, shamming insanity is occasionally resorted to. This might have worked for young Ernest M. Hipple, who killed and robbed an aged woman for only three dollars, had not Pennsylvania's lieutenant governor decided to personally test the slayer's mentality. After doctors had called Hipple a moron, the state official went to, the jail, posed as a convict, and conversed with the murderer. "He could talk as

109

intelligently as the' other prisoners," the lieutenant governor later advised the Board of Pardons hearing the plea for clemency.

Contrary to popular belief, the last meal, consisting of those things requested by the condemned, is not eaten with a great deal of relish—if, in fact, it is eaten at all. Quite often the food is shared with other occupants of the death house. One man ordered for his final supper the delicacies he knew another inmate liked. "Give it to my friend," he said when the meal was brought to him. The recipient of the tray was so pleased that he did the same on the day he was executed.

As the fatal hour approaches, those who smoke usually do so incessantly. They are not permitted to have matches, and keep the guards busy supplying them with lights. It is not uncommon for a man to puff on a cigar or cigarette while being strapped in the chair, and several have continued until the mask went over their faces.

Requests of all sorts are frequently made by prisoners shortly before they pay the supreme penalty. If possible and within reason, these are ordinarily granted. Some of the condemned desire that their worldly goods be disposed of in various ways. A man who strangled a woman to death pleaded that the clothes he wore to prison be burned so that they could not be put on exhibition for the morbidly curious to view. Others ask that farewell notes be delivered to their loved ones. That a carnation be sent to his sweetheart was the last wish of one, while the killer of a sheriff requested a new white shirt to wear in the death chamber. A number have asked for a drink of whisky to ease their going, but I know of no case where it has been given. The state wants murderers to be fully conscious when punishment is meted out to them.

Not long before Sherman L. Strawser was led to the chair for killing a Pennsylvania farmer and robbing him of money with which to buy a wedding dress for the girl he was to marry, he asked his keepers for a Bible. There was nothing out of the ordinary about this, as the condemned often read the Scriptures while in the death cells. For hours, he pored over the pages. Finally, guards heard him mumble, "There, that's it." He had selected the text to be read at his funeral. It was the first three verses of the fourteenth chapter of Job:

Man that is born of a woman is of few days, and full of trouble.

He cometh forth like a flower, and is cut down: he fleeth also as a shadow, and continueth not.

And doth thou open thine eyes upon such an one, and bringest me into judgment with thee?

Strawser also arranged all the details of his burial. Among the pallbearers were four prison guards who had watched over the slayer from the time he was sentenced to die.

The reaction of those on the edge of eternity is often quite different from what might be expected. For instance, a man fainted on hearing the jury's verdict, sobbed for days before his execution, and was certain that he would be unable to walk to the chair. Yet, when the time came, he regained his composure and went bravely and quietly. On the other hand, a hardened criminal who boasted that he had shot down more than one and told the police that he wanted to "burn" was a quaking figure leaning heavily on the arms of guards as he entered the execution room.

Death-chamber speeches are not uncommon. A large number of the condemned make some kind of statement before the lethal current silences them forever. They realize that anything they say, be it only a brief farewell, will be published in the newspapers. It is usually obvious that they have carefully planned and memorized their words. I have seen men come to the chair so frightened that although they had intended to speak, they found it impossible to do so.

As I have said before, those who display outward signs of fear or extreme nervousness in the execution chamber or who must be assisted to the chair are in the minority. But they, as well as those who go with unusual fortitude, create unforgettable scenes.

I was surprised and totally unprepared for the exhibition staged by Michael Alex—called "Death House Mike" because he had escaped the chair five times before he was convicted of a second murder, that of an insurance collector. Alex, whose crime-checkered career started when he was ten and spanned seventeen years, was known as a steel-nerved gunman. Bravado was always present in his many encounters with the law, and he sneered at the first-degree murder verdicts of the juries he faced. He was "tough" and could "take it," the reporters wrote.

But that was before they saw him stagger into Sing Sing's execution chamber, clutching the Roman Catholic prison chaplain to keep from falling. That was before they saw him tremble violently, and heard him sob and cry out hysterically. Gone then was every trace of courage that he may ever have possessed.

Alex managed to control himself until he reached the chair and the priest stepped back. Turning to the witnesses who crowded the chamber, he began protesting his innocence.

"God Almighty," he shrieked, "prove to them that I didn't do it! Why do they accuse me? Why, oh why, do they blame me?"

He stopped for a second to get his breath. Then: "Oh, please, God above in the heavens, I'm innocent. They've accused me of something I never did. I never even saw Ehrlich killed. Please give me a chance, and I know they'll find the guilty party."

Guards started to put him in the chair, but he jerked away. Pointing his finger at the spectators, he yelled:

"Look at those people watching me! They know I'm innocent!"

The shivering little gunman was backed into the chair. He continued to shout as the straps were adjusted and the electrodes applied. I had a little difficulty in getting the helmet in place, as he would not hold his head still.

112

Even the mask did not silence him, and his voice could be heard until I threw the switch. His body lunged against the straps with such force that the heavy one across his stomach broke.

Fortunately for those who participate in executions, cases like that do not occur very often. The more frightened prisoners are supported on their way to the chair, and usually sob, babble incoherently, or pray distractedly. Two have fainted after being strapped in. Rarely, however, do they struggle and carryon as did "Death House Mike."

Sight of the electric chair with its gruesome trappings sometimes causes condemned persons to stop momentarily and gasp–perhaps take a backward step. But only one man in my experience has shown terror as his eyes fell upon it, and he turned as though to run from the room.

A few prisoners about to die will not look at the chair. I remember two men who entered the death chamber with their eyes shut, and did not open them during the entire proceedings. They were Arthur Friedman, who had murdered a New York City detective, and Major Green, a man who had hammered a woman to death.

Friedman, pasty white, stumbled into the room, his eyes closed tightly and his arms outstretched like someone playing blindman's buff. Guards maneuvered him to the chair while he mumbled prayers in Hebrew 'and said weakly, "Good-by." Green shut his eyes when he left his cell, and, assisted by guards, shuffled to his doom without seeing the chair or those in the chamber. I got the impression that he had rehearsed the event in his mind, for, after sitting down, he placed his hands on the arms of the chair, spread his feet apart, and sank back.

Several murderers I have executed were almost insensible figures when they were brought in. Staring straight ahead, they appeared to be wholly unaware of what was taking place. Their movements were as mechanical as a robot's.

When Alfred E. Volckman, twenty-one-year-old killer of a minister's little daughter, was led into Sing Sing's brilliantly illuminated execution chamber, he was like one already dead. He spoke not a word. Although his eyes roved over the witnesses, I doubt that he saw any of them. Guards had to turn him into position on the rubber mat in front of the chair and back him into the seat. He did not blink an eye as he was made ready for the current. Cold water from the head electrode trickled down the back of his neck, but he gave no indication that he felt it. Officially, he died between 11:01 and 11:03 P.M. on February 11, 1937. However, I wonder whether it would not be more accurate to say that he died before then.

The same was true of Robert Roland Lilly, Philadelphia man who was put to death for the slaying of his wife during a quarrel. He acted as though stunned, and did not seem to realize that death for him was but a few seconds away.

Deep despair marked the features of Rudolph Duringer when he was taken to Sing Sing's chair on his twenty-sixth birthday. He had murdered his dancehall sweetheart, and was one of the largest men I have executed. Guided by a keeper, he tottered into the room. His head was sunken on his chest; his eyes, only half open, were riveted on the floor. He dragged himself to the chair, and slumped into it. As he was prepared for the lethal shock, he closed his eyes.

Robert Dreamer, convicted of killing a young girl, was all right until a short time before his execution. Then he began to talk strangely. On his last day, he spoke of writing a letter, but decided to "put it off until tomorrow." He also planned a celebration for his birthday which was three months off. At 12:30 A.M. the guards went for him, and he walked calmly and quietly to Pennsylvania's chair without any apparent understanding of what was to be done to him. Perhaps the fact that more than nine years had passed since his crime was partly responsible for his dazed condition.

Fear is not the only thing that necessitates helping a person to the chair. Physical disability is occasionally responsible. It was the only reason that Joseph Kernerinski was supported by an officer on each side as he traveled "the last mile."

Kemerinski was only twenty, a youth whom life had never treated too kindly. He had been a miner near Wilkes-Barre, Pennsylvania, and, while working one day, his leg had been mangled in an accident. Immediate amputation had been imperative. Upon his recovery, he blamed a local surgeon for the operation which had saved his life, and went to the doctor's office and shot him. The evidence later revealed that he had killed not the man who had performed the operation, but another, thus adding an extra note of horror to the tragedy.

Someone else who required assistance because he had only one leg was John Smith, a man who slew his sweetheart and a friend. His right leg had been lost in army service on the Mexican border. He entered Sing Sing's execution chamber on crutches, which were taken from him when he reached the chair.

Walter Strantz could not have gone to Pennsylvania's electric chair without aid. Before his capture for a barroom murder, he engaged in a gun battle with the police, during which his left heel was shot away. Strantz was unable to walk alone, and hobbled into the execution chamber with his arms around the prison chaplain and the deputy warden. The crippled foot was still bandaged.

Although most condemned prisoners are in no particular hurry to liquidate their debt to society, several have been in a frenzy of haste to get through the ordeal. Alex Kalinowski, who stabbed to death the principal keeper at Auburn Prison because of alleged scanty rations, started to run toward the chair, but guards restrained him.

Silent and self-possessed during his last moments, Raymond Flores, who hurled a young girl from the roof of a New York tenement house, also was anxious for his execution to proceed as quickly as possible. He cooperated with the guards who strapped him in, and did nothing which might delay the throwing of the switch. "If I must go," he had told prison officers that morning, "then hurry me off. I want to get my troubles over with."

Bravado, which is nothing more than imitation courage, I have seen often in the death chamber as wretched men have gone into eternity with a laugh or a quip on their lips. They wanted the world to believe that they were unafraid of death.

One of the most hardened men I have watched die was George Appel, a former Chicago gunman who had slain a New York police lieutenant in a restaurant holdup. The officer, before losing consciousness, had been able to scribble the facts on a sheet of paper. This information led to Appel's arrest and subsequent conviction.

He was scheduled to be executed with two other killers. As all three were regarded as bad actors, they were watched by special guards to prevent any desperate effort to battle their way to freedom. But they caused no trouble, and were comparatively cheerful to the end.

"I committed other crimes," Appel confessed while waiting to be taken to the chair, "but I didn't kill that cop. I wouldn't kill a cop."

The murderer had a sickening smile on his face as he strode through the door of the execution chamber. While the guards were strapping him in, he said, "Well, folks, you'll soon see a baked Appel."

If he had expected anybody present to laugh at the grim jest, he was disappointed. Nothing but complete silence greeted this macabre pun of a man in the last few seconds of his life.

William Deni, murderer of a Philadelphia officer, also tried to be a death-chamber humorist. Sitting down in the chair, the gangster remarked, "I guess the Big Bad Wolf is going to get me."

Unless it is the condemned person himself, I have never seen anyone smile in the death chamber during an execution. Yet, hotheaded Peter Harris, who killed a man he thought had insulted his wife, shouted from the chair to witnesses: "What are you laughing at? There is nothing funny about this. What are you laughing at?" Incidentally, Harris was one of the few who have eaten a hearty last meal.

In January, 1930, two men who were executed for the same crime tried to outdo each other in bravado. They were Frank Plaia, a Brooklyn gang leader, and Michael Sclafoni. They had slain a man and his wife. Once the doomed men had been close friends, but became bitter enemies when each accused the other of the shootings.

Plaia was the first to go. Although he had attempted suicide a few hours earlier, he entered Sing Sing's death chamber with a broad grin on his face. He was chewing gum, and a lighted cigarette was in his hand.

Three minutes later Sclafoni followed. He looked at the chair for several seconds, then ran a finger over its arm. "Dust," he grunted. He asked for a cloth, and was handed one. After wiping off the seat and arms, he remarked disgustedly, "They at least could give a man about to die a clean chair."

For a murder committed during an Auburn Prison riot, three men paid with their lives in the summer of 1930. The trio would not accept religious solace, bragging that they did not need it. All three cursed the witnesses and those in charge of the executions.

The youngest of the three, Jesse Thomas, led the death procession. On entering the chamber, he exclaimed: "Well, well, well! I can walk through and die like a man." Later, in the chair, he called out: "I'll see you all in hell some day. Let 'er go!"

William Force was next. He glanced up at me and said: "I'm all right. What are you so nervous about, boy? Take it easy. I'm in no hurry."

The third man, Claude Udwine, did the most talking. "I want you all to know that I'm doing the simplest thing of my life," he began. "I'm going on an exploring trip. The good part about this thing is that they carry you out—you don't have to walk." When I started to adjust the head electrode, he sneered: "So this is a football game. Oh, well, it's all just a joke. Let's go!"

117

About five years after this triple execution, I put to death one of the toughest criminals I have ever seen. He was Leonard Scarnici, who had fatally shot a detective. On the day he was scheduled to go to the chair, he was whisked to New York City by automobile to attend arguments on a Federal Court writ that would give him a respite. After the judge had denied his application, the gangster said to a newspaper reporter, "Come up to Sing Sing tonight and see a good show, buddy."

At the prison that night, Scarnici, chewing gum and puffing a cigarette, stepped jauntily into the execution room. He made a side remark to an attendant, and sauntered over to the chair. He flopped into it. As guards adjusted the straps, he cautioned: "Not too tight, boys. Take it easy."

Next he addressed Warden Lawes. "Is it O.K., Warden?" he asked.

"He may speak," the warden told the guards. Leaning forward in the chair, Scarnici declared: "All I want to say is this: I want to tell those chiselers in Albany who double-crossed me that I'm a better man than they are. Thank you, Warden." Then to the prison chaplain who accompanied him, "O.K., Father." His cigarette dropped to the floor.

Blowing smoke from a cigar, George Swan, convicted 'with a companion for killing two people in a New York restaurant holdup, swaggered through the death chamber door. In a buttonhole of his shirt was a small pink flower. He seated himself in the chair, took another drag on his cigar, and declared: "It's about time this thing happened. It's been a long time coming. Good-by, everybody." A guard removed the cigar from the prisoner's lips in order to put the mask over his face.

Stephen Ziolkowski, Buffalo gangster, put to double use the cigar which he took with him to the chair. Besides smoking it, he employed it in a last defiant gesture against the society which had doomed him. With a snarl, he hurled the cigar with full force at the witnesses. It struck a stout man in the chest, sending ashes dawn the front of him. "Haw's things, Cap?" the gangster inquired a few seconds later of the guard attaching the leg electrode. Just before I threw the switch, he screamed: "Whoopee, bays! Let'er go!"

Another man who acted in a somewhat similar manner was Frank McBrien, "The Jersey Kid," who was convicted with three others far the slaying of a cashier. He refused the attendance of a clergyman, and, when guards were ready to strap his wrists, flipped his cigarette at the spectators. It hit the leg of a reporter sitting in the front raw.

Witnesses at executions are occasionally the targets far verbal abuse from those on the brink of eternity. Joseph Rado, executed in New Jersey at the same night with McBrien, assailed them. "You spectators, you gate-crashers!" he shouted from the chair.

One night in Sing Sing's death chamber, newspaper-men were partly blamed for sending a person to the chair. The accuser was the condemned youth himself—Joseph Bolognia, trigger man far the sextet who killed a Brooklyn subway collector.

"Where's the newspaper reporters?" he demanded gruffly as he stood beside the chair. There was no answer.

Looking directly at a group he believed represented the press, he continued: "You fellows certainly made a fine mess of things. Why don't you put down what you did? You called me "Tough Tony' and all that. I'm not tough. I've always been a good kid."

As he was being strapped in, he told the officers to send his body to the district attorney who prosecuted him and to the woman who identified him.

I thought he had finished speaking, and started to adjust the helmet. But again he yelled to the reporters: "Put this down, too. I'm innocent. Don't forget that."

Equally bitter and defiant was Joseph O'Loughlin, one of three to die for killing a New York detective in an attempted holdup. The sentences of two others involved in the crime were commuted to life imprisonment. The fact that he had not been spared ired O'Loughlin, and he made it plain just before sitting down in the chair. Then, turning to me, he said, "Let's go, Bob." I admit that I was startled, but managed to hide my surprise. This was the only time a condemned person has addressed me by name in the death chamber. O'Loughlin's last words were in reference to the lethal bolt about to strike him: "Powerful stuff, eh what?"

Nineteen-year-old James Bolger, murderer of a druggist, walked into Sing Sing's execution chamber smiling. "Gentlemen," he said, "I die as I lived–with smile on my face." He continued to smile until a guard stepped forward to put on the black mask.

But I doubt that I have ever seen a more genuine smile in Sing Sing's death chamber than that on the race of Charles Ham, youthful man who had killed and robbed a Brooklyn storekeeper. He kept the promise he had made on the morning of his last day. "I'm not worrying," he had said. "I'll be just the same at the finish as I am now." And he was. Not once did his pleasant expression change as he was prepared for the current, and the smile was still there when his body was removed from the chair. Though Warden Lawes usually does not look at the condemned after they are placed in the chair, for some reason I do not know, his eyes never left Ham during the entire proceedings.

Francis (Two-Gun) Crowley also smiled during the waning seconds of his life, but anyone close to him could tell that it was forced. Crowley had murdered a Long Island cop, after which he took cover in New York City. There he shot it out with the police before his capture. "Hi, Sarge," he called to an officer as he entered the death chamber. In the chair, the youth thanked the warden for all that he had done for him, and sent love to his mother. After the leg electrode had been attached, he pointed to it and said: "The strap isn't tight enough. You'd better fix it."

"I want to make a complaint," declared Charles Fithian as he sat in New Jersey's electric chair. A guard nodded for him to continue. "That soup I had for supper tonight was too hot," the doomed man grumbled.

While I was putting the head electrode on a man in Pennsylvania, he querulously said: "It hurts. You're pinching my ear." I readjusted the helmet to make his last few moments as comfortable as possible, and he commented, "That's better."

Two killers, Frank Negron and Alexander Carrion, wore expressions of mock sadness on their last day of life because clouds hid the sun. "Just our luck," growled the former. "We haven't even got a decent day for it." Carrion retorted, "Well, we can eat, that's what we can." Both ordered large dinners, but lost much of their appetites before the food was brought them.

Apparent indifference to their fate is displayed by a few inmates of the death house prior to and at the time of their executions. Peter Spirellis pleaded guilty to murdering a waitress in Pottsville, Pennsylvania, and showed little interest in his punishment. Patrick O. Downey, slayer of a child, also seemed unconcerned in the death chamber. Guards had to awaken John Davis Jordan half an hour before he was to go, and he still appeared sleepy as he walked uncertainly into Pennsylvania's execution room. He paid little attention to the process of strapping him in.

Bidding farewell to relatives and friends is one of the most difficult things a condemned person does. At least, John Fiorenza, who brutally strangled a woman, found it so. "It was harder to say good-by to Mom than it will be to go to the chair," he told Warden Lawes after his mother had made her last visit. "I feel sorry I caused her all this trouble. She stood by me." He was emotionless and silent when his turn came.

I have never heard any man in the chair actually confess his guilt, but a few have indicated repentance. Others have declared that they died without malice toward anyone, even those who were responsible for their conviction. A number have thanked officials for the kind treatment they received during their imprisonment.

121

Italio Ferdanandi was very much in love with a girl. He talked about her a great deal, and she visited him often in Sing Sing's death house. Her picture was pinned over his heart as he walked into the execution chamber. Before guards strapped his arms, the condemned man lifted his hands in supplication and spoke: "All I have to say is, God forgive me for what I've done. God bless my dear mother and father and sweetheart.'

A prayer for his two children came from the lips of Antonio Peronace just before he was executed. From the chair, the little man who had slain his wife and father-in-law said: "I bless my son seven years old and my daughter. Thanks to God for my daughter."

There was no hatred in the heart of Charles Lovell on the morning that he was executed in Pennsylvania for shooting a man who had insulted his sweetheart. His last words were: "Tell the people of Mount Union I hold nothing against them. I'm dying with a smile. Good-by, all."

The group who watched Sylvester N. Fernandz go to his death in Massachusetts was moved by the doomed prisoner's last request. Fernandz had murdered and robbed a recluse on Christmas Day in order to obtain money with which to buy gifts for his young wife. He walked to the chair without faltering, and, as soon as he was seated, asked permission to shake hands with two friends, a deputy sheriff and a physician, both of whom were in the chamber. The startled warden consented. Fernandz tightly clasped their hands in appreciation for all their kindnesses. Then he resumed his praying.

Some murderers pay the extreme penalty with full willingness. This is either because a clergyman has convinced them that they must give their lives for those they have taken, or because they prefer death to a lifetime behind bars.

One of the first men I was called upon to execute for New York State was a man by the name of William Hoyer. He had slain his wife and five-year-old daughter. Only thirty hours before his death, he had embraced a religious faith. As he sat facing the witnesses, he said calmly: "I wouldn't take ten years, let alone life, to escape this chair. I deserve to go, I ought to go, and I want to go."

Similar sentiments were expressed by Miller Frank Clark, who killed a young girl in Massachusetts because she repulsed his advances. He prepared for his death immediately following his conviction, and told both his spiritual adviser and attorney that he would rather die than spend the rest of his life in prison. During his last days, he asked many questions concerning the mechanics of the chair, the distance he would have to walk, and those who would be in the chamber.

"I'm ready to go, and I deserve it," Peter Kudzinowski said to the principal keeper of the New Jersey State Prison several days before his execution. "If I were freed, I'd probably do the same thing again." Kudzinowski had been convicted of murdering a seven-year-old boy, and had told the authorities that he had killed other children. However, when pressed for details, he would not disclose how and where he had disposed of the bodies. While I was at the switchboard on the night he was executed, a swallow flew into the death chamber from somewhere, circled the room, and went out the door. Two men in death row saw the electrocution because an attendant had inadvertently left the door ajar.

Several times I have put to death brothers or persons otherwise related to each other. But only once has it been necessary for me to send a father and his son into eternity. This was in Massachusetts, and the two were Frank and Anthony DiStasio. They had been convicted of the torch slaying of a Boston laborer in order to collect insurance.

The unusual element in the case was that the father probably could have saved his son. He insisted that the youth was innocent, but refused to sign a statement exonerating him. When questioned as to the reason for his attitude, he told his attorney:

"I love my son better than anything else in the world, and I don't want to leave him behind. He'll be better off dead. I'm going to die happy."

In another cell, the youth indicated that he would gladly shoulder all responsibility for the crime if the governor would spare the older man. "I love my father, and that is why I'm in this predicament," he remarked.

Calm and unassisted, Anthony was brought to the chair first. I thought, perhaps, he might show some sign of bitterness, knowing that his parent had declined to help him. But he did not, and simply said, "Good-by, Father."

The elder DiStasio entered the bare, white room with a firm step. His eyes swept the witnesses, and he said in a clear voice: "Good-by, son. It's tough, but I'll see you again." I believe this man died satisfied. He had taken his son with him.

THREE FAMOUS CASES

Rarely do my friends question me concerning my work and experiences in the death chamber. They realize that it is a subject which I would prefer not to discuss. But a few of them broke their restraint following my three most sensational cases. I refer to the executions of Nicola Sacco and Bartolomeo Vanzetti, Ruth Snyder and Henry Judd Gray, and Bruno Richard Hauptmann.

Several people wanted me to tell them of my observations and any significant details that had failed to find their way into public print. They asked, for example, if Sacco and Vanzetti met their fate as bravely as was reported. What were my emotions when I sent Ruth Snyder into eternity? Did not the fact that she was a woman make my task more difficult? Did Hauptmann in the electric chair provide any indication as to whether he was innocent, or whether he alone was guilty of the revolting crime of which he was convicted?

Naturally, I formed opinions about these cases just as did millions of other people. I followed newspaper stories of the testimony from day to day as the trials proceeded. I also read accounts of the appeals, the pleas for executive clemency, and the final decisions of those in authority. However, when the time came for me to carry out the order of the court in each instance, I did not permit my views to have any effect on the performance of my duty.

The execution of Sacco and Vanzetti was the first in which I was to put to death condemned men in what the public calls a "big case." Sacco, a shoe factory employee, and Vanzetti, a fish peddler, were convicted on July 14, 1921, of murdering Frederick A. Parmenter, a paymaster, and Alexander Berardelli, his guard, at South Braintree, Massachusetts, on April 15, 1920. They had, the state charged, robbed their victims of a shoe factory payroll amounting to more than $15,000.

For six long years, the case dragged through the courts. Appeal after appeal was taken. A legal battle unprecedented in the history of American jurisprudence was waged. Men of prominence, convinced of the two anarchists' innocence, cried "Persecution!" Radical and liberal organizations throughout the world politically exploited the case until it became of far-reaching importance.

After Governor Alvan T. Fuller announced on August 3, 1927, that Sacco and Vanzetti must die, and it was known that I would officiate at the execution, I prepared myself for a flood of threats. Since I had received such notes in connection with cases that had attracted little or no public attention, I surely expected many protests from sympathizers of the two men. But, strangely enough, not a single threat against my life or the lives of my family reached me.

I made one unnecessary trip to the Massachusetts State Prison at Charlestown. This was on August 10, the day on which the governor's reprieve of June 29 expired. I had spent the night before at the home of my daughter, Frances, who feared for my safety. As I was leaving, she called after me to be careful.

Arriving in Boston, I was met at the South Station by the prison's chief engineer. We took a taxi to the penitentiary, going through the railroad freight yards to the service gate in order to avoid newspaper reporters and photographers and the crowd that had already gathered in the vicinity. Later in the afternoon, I was escorted to the death chamber, where I was left alone. Keys to the gate leading to the yard were given me, and, for this consideration, I was to act as "turnkey."

Most of my time was spent in preparing the chair for the grisly business ahead. Dinner time came and passed— but no food for me. After inquiring of an officer if I was to be fed, a tray was brought from the warden's house. In the excitement, I had been entirely forgotten.

As darkness fell, the air seemed charged with electricity. Everybody in the prison, from the warden down, was uneasy, tense. Outside, there were great crowds and noisy demonstrations. Scores of policemen, many of them mounted, attempted to control the throng and the traffic jam of hundreds of automobiles. Never before had a penal institution been so armed and garrisoned.

I do not deny that I was nervous. I knew that the eyes of the world were on Boston that night; that the least thing out of the ordinary or the slightest mishap in the death chamber would be inflated into a sensation that might result in serious repercussions. I inspected and reinspected the apparatus to make sure it was ready and functioning properly.

Word was brought to me shortly after eleven o'clock that the execution had been postponed. Governor Fuller had granted a last-hour reprieve through August 22 to allow a ruling by a Supreme Court justice on an application for a writ of error. It was good news to the thousands milling around the prison and the millions of people in all parts of the earth who were hoping that Sacco and Vanzetti would be spared. I left the prison, and hurried to a hotel, where I spent the rest of the night.

On August 22, I reported at the prison in midafternoon, and went through the same procedure as before. Again excitement ran high. As the hands of the clock neared midnight, many nerves were almost at the breaking point. The death march began three minutes after twelve.

Few people recall that Celestino F. Madeiros, a young Portuguese who had killed a bank cashier and had won seven respites, preceded Sacco and Vanzetti to the chair

127

that night. No political cry had been raised over him; no committee had been organized for his defense; no petitions had been signed in his behalf. He had been practically friendless during his entire imprisonment.

With a guard on each side, Madeiros entered the death chamber in a semi-stupor, said to have been caused by overeating. Looking straight ahead, he walked quickly to the chair and sat down. He spoke not a word. At 12:09, he was pronounced dead, and his body was removed. Then they went after Sacco, whose cell was next to that of Madeiros.

Sacco trod "the last mile" slowly but steadily. He was unaccompanied by a clergyman, having earlier refused spiritual consolation from the prison chaplain. As he stepped into the room, I noticed that he was deathly pale. It was obvious that he was under a terrific mental strain. Without support, he made his way to the chair. While guards were strapping him in and the electrodes were being applied, he shouted in his native Italian, "Long live anarchy!"

Everything was now ready except the placing of the mask over his face. But the mask could not be found. The guards and I searched frantically for it. I could feel beads of perspiration starting out on my forehead. Meanwhile, Sacco continued to speak.

"Farewell, my wife and child and all my friends," he cried in broken English. He had two children, a boy and a girl, and his difficulty with our language, together with the torture he was undergoing, probably accounted for the use of the singular instead of the plural of "child."

The condemned man next addressed all who were in the room. "Good evening, gentlemen," he said. His last words were, "Farewell, Mother."

As Sacco was saying these things, a guard strode back into the room with the mask. It had been caught in Madeiros' clothing, and carried from the chamber when his body was taken out for autopsy. Had it not been for Sacco's talking, the incident might have been noticed. As it was, the only reporter present failed to observe what had happened, and no mention was made of it in the newspapers. I have often since been thankful that the little Italian was so talkative as he sat in the chair awaiting the end.

Vanzetti was the most composed of the three who died that night. He, also, was unattended by a minister. When guards came for him, he shook their hands, and kept in step with them to the door of the execution chamber.

"I want to thank you for everything you have done for me, Warden," he said to Warden Hendry, firmly clasping him by the hand. The warden was deeply moved, and made no reply.

To the witnesses, Vanzetti directed his next words. "I wish to tell you I am innocent, and never committed any crime, but sometimes some sin. I thank you for everything you have done for me. I am innocent of all,' crime, not only of this, but all. I am an innocent man.

Before I threw the switch, he spoke again. "I wish to forgive some people for what they are now doing to me."

Thus did the curtain drop on the case that rocked the world.

A large crowd was still outside the prison when left in a taxi. Only a few people recognized me, and one man shouted, "There he goes!" But no attempt was made to stop or to follow me. In my hotel room, I chatted a while with a friend. He advised me to be on guard until I was out of Boston.

"Feeling ran pretty high tonight," he said. "There were some out there who'd do almost anything the way they felt. I think you ought to have police protection.

"Not me," I replied, and we changed the subject. Although demonstrations continued for hours afterward, no one disturbed me. I returned to my home the next day.

Ruth Snyder was the first woman I was called upon to execute. She was also the first woman to die in Sing Sing's chair since the electrocution of Mrs. Martha Place in 1899. Mrs. Snyder and her paramour, Henry Judd Gray, had been convicted of the slaying of her art-editor husband in the Snyder home in Queens Village, New York, on the night of March 20, 1927. It had been a brutal murder. The couple had beaten and strangled the unsuspecting man while he slept. The motive was to get his life insurance.

There was every dement in the case to inflame the imagination of the newspaper-reading public that enjoys such sensations—love, hate, the ancient triangle. Ruth Snyder was painted as an attractive blonde who had reduced the weak-willed Judd Gray to the status of her slave. Column upon column was devoted to the details of the three-week trial, the condemned pair's agonizing days in the death house, and the unsuccessful attempts to save their lives. Public interest, fed by these lurid accounts in the press, bordered on hysteria.

A few weeks before the execution, two stories about me started going the rounds. One was to the effect that I was so horrified at the thought of putting a woman to death that my health had become impaired, and that I intended to refuse the assignment. The other was that I planned to appeal to Governor Smith to spare Mrs. Snyder. Neither, of course, was true.

However, so much credence was placed in the first rumor that I received letters from many individuals offering to substitute for me. "The electric chair is too good for her, and I am willing to do the job," a man in New York City assured me. A woman in Kingston, New York, wrote me as follows:

I saw in the news that you just did not care to execute Mrs. Snyder. If you don't want to do it, will you let me have first offer? I won't mind it one bit to execute Mrs. Snyder. It is just what she should get, the chair. I could execute Ruth Snyder with a good heart and think I had done a good deed. I think, Mr. Elliott, if they did have a woman executioner for the same states you have, it would be no more than right to have a woman to execute a woman, and that would take a whole lot off your mind. If you would like to have me help you the night the two are put in the chair, I will be more than glad to do so. I hope to hear from you soon.

130

I did not reply to that letter any more than I attempted to correct the story that I would intercede for the murderess. I have never been asked to plead for any condemned person whom I was to execute, and should I be, I most certainly would refuse.

Although there was strong public sentiment against the two slayers, especially the woman, a surprisingly large number of threats were sent me both before and after the execution. Several warned that if I were Ruth Snyder's executioner, vengeance would be wreaked on my daughters. Only two or three of the writers were concerned about the fate of Gray. Except for those aimed at my children, these threats did not worry me, and none were turned over to the police.

The fact that a man and a woman were to die together for a crime which had been inspired by an illicit love brought Warden Lawes more than fifteen hundred applications from anxious would-be witnesses. About one hundred and twenty-five newspapers and news services sought press privileges in the death chamber. Due to the smallness of the room, it was impossible to grant more than twenty such requests.

On January 12, 1928, the date set for the double execution, I spent the afternoon in New York City, later driving to Sing Sing with a physician. A curious, morbid crowd had gathered outside the prison entrance when I arrived. The throng grew as the evening wore on. An estimated two hundred automobiles were parked along the thoroughfare leading to the main gates of the "big house." The scene was not unlike an election night, except that the people were not noisy. They talked in low voices.

At the prison, I was asked whether Ruth Snyder's hair should be cut so that the head electrode could do its deadly work more quickly and efficiently. She had always combed her hair with feminine pride in its appearance. Moreover, I learned that it had grown thin during her months of imprisonment. I told them that it would be unnecessary to touch it.

131

In the death chamber a short time later, I made the usual preparations. I had brought my own electrodes for use on Mrs. Snyder. While I awaited the arrival of the officers and the witnesses, a feeling of repulsion swept over me. I was to send a woman, a mother, into eternity. The more I permitted my mind to dwell upon it, the more it cut deep into my heart. But I also realized that this woman had murdered; that the law demanded her life for the one she had so cruelly taken.

Wearing a brown smock over a black, knee-length calico skirt, Ruth Snyder was led into the death chamber at exactly 11:01 o'clock. She was preceded by the Reverend John P. McCaffrey, Roman Catholic prison chaplain, and was borne up by a matron on each side. Her blonde hair had been freshly combed. Her chin was held high, but it trembled. She faltered as she attempted to repeat the words of a prayer after the priest.

When her eyes fell upon the instrument of death, she almost collapsed. The matrons tenderly assisted her to the chair, and, as she was placed in it, she bro down and wept. "Jesus, have mercy on me, for I have sinned," she prayed between sobs.

The matrons moved away. Guards quickly adjusted the straps. One applied an electrode to her right leg on which the black cotton stocking had been rolled down to the ankle. I parted her hair at the back of the neck to permit the sponge of the other electrode come in contact with the flesh. Then I affixed the head piece. While all this was going on, I thought I hear, her mumble that she was innocent. Her next words were distinct: "Father, forgive them, for they know not what they do."

The mask went over her face, and she uttered an-other prayer. "Jesus, have mercy," she cried pitifully, pleadingly. I stepped to the controls. After looking at the chair, I threw the switch. The body of this life-loving young woman stiffened under the straps. There was complete silence in the room, except for the crackling, sputtering sound of the current.

I glanced at the witnesses in the rows of pew-like seats. Most of them were pale. I knew that some had viewed other executions calmly—but the sight of a woman in death's embrace was proving too much for them. Near the rear door stood Warden Lawes. His eyes were glued to the floor, and not once did he raise them during the entire proceedings.

As the current surged through Ruth Snyder's body, I thought of her mother and little daughter, Lorraine. My sympathies were more with them than with the woman in the chair. They were innocent of any wrongdoing, yet upon them had been brought disgrace and untold suffering. They, together with Judd Gray's family, were the real victims of this heart-rending tragedy.

After about two minutes, I turned off the current. The prison physician, Dr. Sweet, stepped forward, applied his stethoscope for a few seconds, and pronounced the woman dead. The body was lifted from the chair, and wheeled into the autopsy room.

Judd Gray, attended by the Reverend Anthony N. Peterson, Protestant chaplain, followed in a few minutes. He was clad in a gray suit and white shirt. On his feet were felt slippers. Gone were the horn-rimmed glasses which had become so familiar. Because of the mask, it had been necessary for him to remove these before leaving his cell.

With firm, quick step, the condemned man walked straight to the chair. He sat down without any assistance, and prayed silently. I got the impression that he was willing, even anxious, to pay his debt to society. He was one of the bravest men I have ever seen go to death by law.

There was pity in my heart for Judd Gray when I threw the switch to end his life. I felt extremely sorry for this man who had forsaken his wife and daughter for the woman who lay dead a short distance away. I believe nearly everyone in the room did.

Shortly after the execution was over, I left the prison for home. My wife was waiting up for me, but she asked no questions. Though it was very late, I read for an hour before going to bed. I wanted to erase the thought of my night's work.

The next day I was surprised to see on the front page of a New York City tabloid an actual photograph of Ruth Snyder in the electric chair. Unknown to the prison officials, a newspaper photographer had snapped the picture while the lethal current was coursing through the woman's body. A rather ingenious method had been employed to accomplish the feat. To the man's left ankle had been strapped a small camera, which was concealed by his wide trouser leg. The camera was manipulated by a plunger in the operator's trouser pocket. By reaching the death chamber ahead of the other witnesses, the photographer had managed to get a front-row seat, and took the picture when no one was looking. This incident led to the searching of witnesses at all future executions at Sing Sing.

It was, indeed, a horrible picture, but a grimly realistic and truthful record of how Ruth Snyder died. The ethics of taking or printing a photograph of this sort is not for me to discuss. However, I am inclined to believe that if more such pictures were published with the permission of the authorities, the homicide rate might decrease. Public opinion might also be aroused to the extent that capital punishment would be abolished. In either event, I think their publication would be fully justified.

With the execution of Mrs. Snyder and her lover, the case ended for those who had been associated with it. But not for me. Stories, some of them purported interviews, appeared concerning the role I played. One in particular, printed in the magazine section of a now extinct New York City newspaper, described me as having been semi-hysterical that night when, of all nights, a steady hand and nerve were essential. After the execution, the paper said, I was on the verge of prostration, and kept brushing my hands before my eyes, as if to drive away a specter. At home, it continued, I was put under the care of a doctor, who found it necessary to administer sedatives

134

in order to quiet me. The story added, supposedly quoting me: "All the night—and to this day—Ruth Snyder's face keeps appearing before me. I am haunted by her, appealing to me for mercy—mercy I couldn't give!"

Several citizens complained about this article to Governor Smith. They were under the impression that the piece had been printed with my knowledge and consent; and that I had permitted my feelings to be paraded for purposes of sensationalism. The Department of Correction, disturbed by what had happened, immediately communicated with me. I explained the facts, and the matter was closed. But similar stories continue to be published from time to time in newspapers and magazines, and cause me no little annoyance and indignation.

The world was shocked by the news that Charles Augustus Lindbergh, Jr., twenty-month-old son of the famous flier, had been kidnapped from his home near Hopewell, New Jersey, on the night of March 1, 1932. It was enraged when it learned that, in spite of payment of the demanded $50,000 ransom, the baby had been slain. Finding of the body in a clump of bushes about three miles from the Lindbergh estate on May 12 started the greatest manhunt in modern times.

For nearly two and a half years, federal and state authorities searched for the person or persons who had committed this inhuman crime. Every clue, every tip was carefully investigated. When it began to look as though the kidnaper-murderer might go unpunished, there was a "break" in the case. On September 15, 1934, a man paid for some gas at a New York City filling station with a ten-dollar gold certificate. The salesman, unaccustomed to receiving that type of bill, became suspicious, and on impulse jotted down on the note the license number of the car. A visit to a bank revealed that the money was a Lindbergh ransom bill. The man who had passed it was Bruno Richard Hauptmann, a Bronx, New York, carpenter.

135

Hauptmann was not arrested immediately. Police trailed him for several days while he continued spending the "hot" money. Then they nabbed him. In his garage were uncovered nearly $15,000 more of the ransom cash and other damning evidence. The German was promptly indicted for murder, and went on trial at Flemington, New Jersey, on January 2, 1935, amid carnival-like scenes. On February 13, after eleven hours of deliberation, a jury of eight men and four women convicted him. There was no recommendation for mercy. Supreme Court Justice Thomas Trenchard sentenced Hauptmann to die in the week of March 18; but the execution was automatically stayed when defense attorneys carried the case to the Court of Errors and Appeals. The high tribunal unanimously upheld the verdict the following October 9, and the week of January 13, 1936, was then set for the electrocution.

I first entered the picture on January 4, 1936, when Colonel Mark O. Kimberling, principal keeper of the New Jersey State Prison at Trenton, telephoned me that I was to put Hauptmann to death at eight P.M. on January 17. From that moment on, I worried a great deal. In fact, I dreaded this assignment more than any other. I had read the voluminous testimony of the witnesses and experts, the summations of the lawyers, and the charge of the judge. Friends who attended sessions of the trial had given me their impressions of the case. The evidence had been largely circumstantial. Though it was generally believed that more than one person was implicated in the crime, none but Hauptmann had been found. I wondered whether justice would best be served by snuffing out the life of this man.

On the afternoon of January 16, Governor Harold G. Hoffman granted a reprieve. Hauptmann's death was then scheduled for the week of March 30. Colonel Kimberling informed me that it would be on Tuesday, March 31, at which time one Charles Zied would also be executed. Zied, however, received a last-minute stay, and did not go to the chair until the following June.

136

Two representatives of a certain news syndicate sought me out following announcement of the new date for Hauptmann's execution. They tried to bargain with me for what would have been a trifling effort on my part. They wanted me to press a secretly installed electric button as soon as Hauptmann entered the death chamber, again when he was seated in the chair, and once more at the instant I turned on the current. They assured me that it could be accomplished without detection, but they did not disclose how they expected to get the wires into the execution room without the knowledge of the prison authorities. Needless to say, I gave their offer not a second's consideration.

But my curiosity was aroused. I asked the men why they were willing to pay so much and go to such trouble for these signals. They explained that it was to be first with the news. Approximately six minutes would elapse between the time that Hauptmann would be led into the death chamber and the instant he would be pronounced dead and the witnesses and reporters would be free to leave. Had I agreed to the proposed arrangement, their particular newspaper and syndicate would have had at least a six-minute beat on the opposition with this big "spot" news story. That, they informed me, would be worth a large sum of money.

A day or so later, a man whose name and affiliation I did not learn managed in some way to obtain my privately listed telephone number, and called me. He had a similar proposition.

"I have in my pocket a check for $10,000 made out to you, Mr. Elliott," he said, "and, with that in mind, I should like to talk with you regarding a small service you can render my organization on the night Hauptmann goes to the chair. There will be no risk whatever to you or your reputation."

I told him that I was not interested, and that he should not attempt to communicate with me again. I hung up the receiver, and heard no more from him.

As in the Snyder-Gray case, threats and vituperations arrived in every mail. "If you give B. R. H. the juice," wrote one person, "you will be sorry. You will pay as much for it as he does, for he is not guilty." Another letter, signed "A Friend of Hauptmann," read:

You may think this very impudent of me. You may also overlook it and say that I am a silly little child, but I will say this: if you execute Bruno Richard Hauptmann, then I hope that all your life it shall come back to you and haunt you. I am sure that in your heart you will always know that you are no better than a murderer, for you will be one.

I think now, and I always shall, that Hauptmann is innocent, and that if someone would go deeper into Dr. Condon's testimony and also the Lindbergh's, they would find that there is a lot that should be told that wasn't. You are going to forget this letter probably, but I hope not, for I would like for this whole world to see so they shall know how I feel about it. Please do all that is possible to free Hauptmann. If you won't think of him, think of his son and his wife and all the people who love him.

Newspaper reporters hounded me for days in the hope of getting some kind of statement. I could not set foot outside the house without running into them. How I would be able to elude them on March 31 was a problem. My daughter, Frances, suggested a ruse to pull them off the scent. She would drive her car up to the front door of our home, giving the impression that I was to leave with her. Meanwhile, I would go out the back way.

The plan worked perfectly. A friend drove me to the railroad station, and from there I went to New York City. I was met by one of my sons-in-law, who accompanied me to Trenton by train. On arrival at the state capital, I was picked up by a car sent by the prison.

A curious crowd started to gather early on the streets surrounding the institution. Newsreel cameramen, radio announcers, and newspaper people swarmed about the entrance. Local and state police maintained order. The excitement was very much like that at Boston on the night when Sacco and Vanzetti were put to death.

Shortly before seven o'clock, I went to the execution room. Before being permitted to enter, officers searched me from head to foot. It was the first time that this had happened to me, but I submitted willingly. I realized that the prison authorities could not afford to take chances on anyone's sneaking such forbidden articles as cameras, weapons, and bottles into the death chamber.

Eight o'clock came, but the witnesses were not brought in. Minutes passed, and still there was no sign of activity. I began to wonder whether Hauptmann's life had been spared. After what seemed a long time, I was informed that Colonel Kimberling had postponed the execution for at least forty-eight hours pending a grand jury investigation.

On Friday, April 3, the day of the execution, Mrs. Elliott and I left the house at seven A.M. before the reporters and photographers had begun their daily vigil. I had borrowed the license plates from my son's car, as newspapermen knew mine and were using them to check on my movements. We drove to Summit, New Jersey, and spent the morning with friends.

At one P.M., I telephoned the prison, and was instructed to proceed to Trenton. I did so, and on the suggestion of an official, stopped at the outskirts of the city to leave my car. In the garage where I waited for someone from the penitentiary, the talk was all of Hauptmann and the forthcoming execution.

"He's guilty, all right," commented a mechanic.

"You bet," chimed in another man standing near by. "I'd like to have the job of that fellow, Elliott, when he turns on the juice tonight. It would be a pleasure."

"Maybe you wouldn't feel that way if you really had the job," I told him. He did not, of course, know who I was.

I reached the prison about four P.M. The procedure of three days before was followed again. Canvas was hung from the three-foot-high rope which separates the witnesses from the chair. This barrier was to prevent anyone from taking a photograph of Hauptmann's last struggles.

It was a cold, blustery night, so the crowd in the vicinity of the prison was smaller than on my first trip. But even then the police had all they could do to manage the throng. As each witness or an individual on official business arrived, his credentials were carefully scrutinized, and he was thoroughly frisked.

Shortly before the fateful hour of eight o'clock, a guard entered the execution room. He had just come from death row.

"How are things back there?" I inquired.

"Exactly as I expected," he replied. "His attorney has told him that there isn't a chance for him, but he won't believe it. He thinks something will turn up the last minute to save him. And there might at that."

The hands of the clock pointed to eight, then eight ten, eight twenty, eight thirty. Still nothing happened in the death chamber, and Hauptmann lived on. No word reached me as to what was delaying the execution.

"I guess he was right," I remarked to "the guard as my wrist watch showed eight thirty-five.

"It looks that way," he agreed.

Just then the door opened, and, preceded by Colonel Kimberling, the witnesses filed in. There were approximately fifty of them—newspapermen, physicians, members of the New Jersey Legislature, state policemen, and a representative of Governor Hoffman. I have never seen a more orderly group of witnesses, unless it was on the night that Mrs. Mary Frances Creighton and Everett C. Appelgate, her partner in crime, died in Sing Sing's electric chair.

A guard held up a large clock by which the execution could be timed. Colonel Kimberling ordered an assistant to telephone the central office, and ascertain whether there was any message. While this man was gone, Colonel Kimberling addressed the witnesses. He warned them against any movements during the proceedings, and insisted on absolute silence.

"If Hauptmann has anything to say, I'll hear it," he declared. "If you don't hear it, I'll tell you about it

140

afterward. But no matter what happens, I don't want a move out of anyone. It will be to everybody's advantage to obey the rules."

I then tested the chair by illuminating the electric light bulbs on the wooden board which lay across the arms of the death seat. By this time, the assistant had returned. There had been no message. Colonel Kimberling nodded to a guard, who disappeared through the door leading to the death cells. A hush fell over the room, broken only by an occasional cough.

In a few seconds, the door opened. The guard entered first, followed by the condemned man's two spiritual advisers, the Reverend John Matthiesen and the Reverend D. G. Werner. One of them was reading aloud from the Bible; the other was offering a prayer. Hauptmann was right behind them. His head, which had been shaved, tilted slightly to one side. His face was yellow; his features were drawn. He was wearing a gray-blue shirt, open at the neck, and khaki trousers with dark stripes along the side. He glanced neither to the right nor to the left. He walked past the chair, and would have collided with a physician had not a guard stopped him. The guard turned him around, and maneuvered him to the chair. He gripped its broad arms with his hands, staring straight ahead as he was strapped in. His lips did not move, and he gave no indication that he wished to speak. I placed the head electrode on him, and helped to adjust the mask. At precisely 8:44 o'clock, I was given the signal. The current streaked through the condemned man.

While I operated the controls, I could picture Hauptmann's aged mother in far-off Germany, sitting in an armchair and watching the clock. She was hoping and praying that his life would be spared. Whether guilty or not, he was her son. My heart went out to her, as it has to so many other mothers whose sons I have had to execute.

Much has been made of the fact that Hauptmann maintained his silence to the end. That mayor may not have been intentional. When this man went to his death, he was a bewildered, almost insensible figure. As eight o'clock passed and the minutes lengthened into half an hour, he probably concluded that he had been given another lease on life. It had happened before, so why was it not reasonable to assume that it had happened again? But then the guard came for him, and told him that it was time to go. He found it unbelievable. He was stunned. Before he could collect his wits, he was in the death chamber and in the chair. I believe it would have been impossible for Hauptmann to have expressed himself with any clarity even if he had had something of vital importance to say.

Not long after the execution, a well-known newspaper columnist and radio commentator reported that had been seen in a New York night club chatting with Governor Hoffman. He implied that we had met so that I could impart to New Jersey's chief executive some inside information concerning Hauptmann's last minutes on earth. This story was completely without foundation. I never met any figure in the Hauptmann case. Moreover, the governor would have had no reason for wanting to talk with me. As I mentioned before, he had had a representative in the death chamber, and this man had told him of everything that happened. There was nothing I could have added.

WOMEN IN THE CHAIR

It seems to be the popular impression that women are braver than men in meeting death, that they are more likely to accept their fate calmly and stoically. My observation as executioner leads me to question that.

Generally speaking, condemned women are pitiful figures in the death chamber. They are sometimes on the verge of collapse and require physical support. That they are under severe mental strain is ordinarily apparent.

Of the five women I have sent into eternity, only one was unafraid. For the others, I believe that death held indescribable terrors—terrors which they tried to conceal from those who watched them die.

As I have said before, Ruth Snyder was visibly shaken by fear when she went to the chair. But at least she managed to walk "the last mile." In the case of Mrs. Mary Frances Creighton, it was necessary to carry her to her doom, thereby presenting one of the most ghastly scenes in my experience.

Mrs. Creighton was called a modern Lucrezia Borgia. How she came by this title is revealed by a study of her amazing career. In 1923, she was tried in New Jersey for the poison-murder of her brother, Raymond Avery, who had a legacy and some life insurance which would be hers on his death. Sitting in court with her recently born son, she hardly looked like one who would kill her own kin. There was indisputable proof that she had purchased arsenic just before her brother's fatal attack; but no one who might have seen her administer the lethal dose could be produced. She was acquitted in short order.

Soon after that, Mrs. Creighton was indicted for doing away with her husband's parents. First she was put on trial for murdering her mother-in-law. This time the jury decided that the amount of arsenic found in the body of the woman was not sufficient to cause death. The state did not bother to prosecute the other indictment.

After moving from place to place in their flight from the past, the Creightons finally settled down in Baldwin, New York. They became acquainted with a family by the name of Appelgate, who eventually moved in with them. Late in 1935, Mrs. Creighton and Everett C. Appelgate were charged with the slow and deliberate murder by poisoning of the latter's buxom and unwanted wife, Ada. The motive, it was alleged, was to free Appelgate so he could marry Mrs. Creighton's fifteen-year-old daughter, Ruth, whom he had seduced. On the witness stand, Mrs. Creighton did an unusual thing. She confessed to the crime, but dragged Appelgate down with her. He knew all about the plot, she swore, and assisted her in feeding poisoned eggnogs to Mrs. Appelgate. After that, there could have been but one verdict.

During her first few months in the death house, the murderess bore up comparatively well. Perhaps she thought that she would escape paying the extreme penalty that she would again outwit the law. However, from the time she learned that the Court of Appeals had unanimously affirmed her conviction and Appelgate's, she was seized by fear, and suffered from major hysteria. Her condition grew worse as the days passed.

Those weeks immediately preceding Mrs. Creighton's execution on July 16, 1936, were torturous ones for her. She ate almost nothing, her nourishment consisting of little more than ice cream. She also refused to exercise. When not weeping, she was moaning or praying. Many a night she never closed her eyes, staring up at the ceiling from her cell cot. She often dreamed of the fate that awaited her, and would wake up screaming, "I can't stand it, I can't stand it!"

In the period that Mrs. Creighton was at Sing Sing, I executed ten men there. She knew when each of them went. It was impossible, under existing conditions, to keep that news and some of the details from her. The slamming of a door, loud talking, or a scream—each took on a horrible significance to her on those nights. Once or twice on such occasions, she fainted.

I am sure that Mrs. Creighton died bit by bit with each of those men. The approach of that day when her own life was to be ended found her bedridden and partially paralyzed. She moved with difficulty, and could hardly speak above a whisper. So serious was her condition reported that, two days before the scheduled execution, Governor Herbert H. Lehman named a special medical commission of five to give the woman a thorough physical and mental examination. After a two-hour test, the group informed the governor:

We find no evidence of organic disease of the central nervous system or of the body as a whole. Mrs. Creighton is well developed, well nourished, and muscular. If she has lost weight, it is not apparent. Her disturbances in motor power, in sensation, and in speech are in part hysterical. They are grossly exaggerated by conscious malingering. Her mind appears to be clear, and she fully appreciates her present situation.

She is suffering from a type of disability which would improve rapidly if she were encouraged, and get worse if she is discouraged. Her condition is the reaction to the situation in which she finds herself.

Without comment, the governor made public the commission's report. When I heard this announced over the radio, I was convinced that, barring unforeseen developments, there would be no executive clemency for Mrs. Creighton. I drove to Ossining the following night, and, as a crowd had gathered at the main entrance of the prison, I went in by another gate. There I was told that the condemned woman had completely collapsed, and was being attended by physicians. Because of her condition, she was to be wheeled into the execution chamber.

When a woman and one or more men are to be executed on the same night, the woman invariably goes first. This is to spare her the ordeal of waiting. In this instance, Warden Lawes originally intended that Appelgate should lead the death procession, because if Mrs. Creighton were to precede the man, she would have to pass the cell in which he was confined. However, at the request of Governor Lehman, the order was changed. That afternoon there had been an unsuccessful attempt to get Mrs. Creighton to assume full blame for the crime, and it was thought that she might say something on the way to the chair which would save her partner.

"I'm afraid you're in for some trouble tonight," an officer warned me as I prepared the apparatus. "She's going to be hard to handle."

I had read newspaper accounts of Mrs. Creighton's ailments and apparent helplessness. I knew that she was terrified at the thought of death, and had been that way for a long time. I steeled myself for what I believed was going to be a difficult case.

At the appointed hour, Mrs. Creighton was wheeled into the stuffy room—the first person in the history of Sing Sing thus to be conveyed to his doom. Due to her pathetic state, she was wearing the pink crepe nightgown and black satin kimono which had been her attire earlier in the day. Black bedroom slippers were on her feet. A rosary rested in her lap.

As the wheel chair was placed alongside the electric chair, I glanced at the woman. Her head drooped limply. Her dark hair, which had become streaked with gray during her imprisonment, was disheveled. Her face was a sickening yellow; her eyes were closed. It was obvious that she was unconscious.

Guards in their shirt sleeves lifted Mrs. Creighton into the high-backed death seat, and held her while the straps and electrodes were quickly applied. The rosary fell to the concrete floor with a clatter. I pressed her head back against the rubber headrest and secured it there. Not once during this procedure did she show the slightest sign of animation. I felt as though I were about to electrocute a person already dead, so lifeless did she seem.

Two matrons and several guards stood in front of the chair. There were two reasons for this: the first was as a precaution against photographers; the second, to shield the dying woman as much as possible from the view of the male witnesses. When I threw the switch, the matrons turned their faces away. One put her head on the shoulder of the other, and wept silently.

I have always believed that accompanying a woman into the death chamber and remaining throughout the execution a most trying ordeal for the matrons. For months, they have been the almost constant companions of the person under sentence of death, and, unless the prisoner is especially unruly or disagreeable, they can hardly resist becoming sympathetic. At one execution, a matron became so upset that she had to be led from the room.

To say that it was a distasteful task to execute a woman in Mrs. Creighton's condition is an understatement. But it would have been more revolting—certainly more difficult for me—had she been conscious and created an unpleasant scene. As it was, she was spared any death-chamber torture, and caused no trouble for those who officiated.

I could not help but observe the similarity of this case to that of Ruth Snyder and Judd Gray. Particularly noticeable were the witnesses' sympathy for the man and their lack of feeling for the woman.

It was reported the next day that the prison authorities had mercifully eased Mrs. Creighton's path to the chair. They had, it was said, given her a hypodermic injection of morphine shortly before her execution, thereby inducing the coma. Whether or not this was true, I cannot say. I have never inquired.

A week after Mrs. Creighton's execution, I went to Sing Sing again. In the death chamber, I saw that one of the guards had a forearm bandaged. I asked him what had happened. The officer explained that he had been severely burned while lifting Mrs. Creighton's body from the chair. Previously, he had been able to protect himself with the heavy clothing worn by the condemned person, but the woman's garments had been too flimsy. His arm had come in contact with her unusually hot flesh. The resulting burn had sent him to the hospital for treatment.

My attention was called not long ago to articles by Ruth Creighton in a national magazine. She told in graphic detail of her unhappy girlhood, of her illicit relationship with Appelgate, and of the chain of circumstances that finally led to murder. She concluded her tragic story by stating that nearly two years after her mother's death, she accidentally met me. Without knowing who I was, she shook my hand and talked with me. Imagine our embarrassment when our identities were disclosed to each other, she wrote.

Perhaps that made a dramatic end to a story. A macabre touch of irony, Ruth Creighton caned it. But it was purely fictional. I have never seen or talked with the girl. Neither have I met a relative of any other person whom I have executed. Once, following an electrocution, I waited inside the prison for some time just to avoid the possibility of such a meeting. Two sisters of the dead man were outside, and did not leave until an officer compelled them to do so.

Few condemned prisoners have undergone greater mental suffering than Mrs. Anna Antonio. Three times she was virtually snatched from the brink of eternity. Three times she had been ready to die, only to have her life prolonged for a short while by a reprieve. She finally lost her long and desperate fight, and paid the supreme penalty at Sing Sing on August 9, 1934.

Mrs. Antonio's crime was planning the murder of her husband, Salvatore, a dope peddler. She had, the state charged, conspired with Sam Faraci and Vincent Saetta to kill him on Easter morning, 1932, for his $5,300 life insurance. All three were convicted, and doomed to the chair.

Fifteen months passed before the sentence of the court was carried out. During this period, Sing Sing's electric chair took twenty-four lives. On four different occasions, I executed as many as three men on the same night. This must have been nerve-shattering to Mrs. Antonio, who, like Mrs. Creighton, was aware of each time a man marched to his death.

The Court of Appeals having upheld the verdict, I was notified to report at the prison on June 28, 1934, for the execution of the woman and her two accomplices. My wife accompanied me to Ossining that night, as we had planned to leave early the next morning for a short vacation in Western New York. I reached the death chamber a little early, and made the customary inspection of the equipment and tested the chair. The officers and doctors arrived at the usual hour. We waited for eleven o'clock.

Eleven o'clock came, but the witnesses were not ushered in. Minutes passed—an hour—two hours. Still there were no signs that the execution was to proceed. Two or three times I heard a car drive into the prison yard and stop at the death house. This indicated to us that something out of the ordinary was happening. However, no word reached us as to what was taking place or why there was a delay.

At 1: 15 A.M.—two hours and a quarter after the time set for the execution—the principal keeper entered the death chamber He announced that we could leave, but should return the following night. Governor Lehman had granted a twenty-four-hour stay.

What had resulted in the last-minute respite was this: just before eleven o'clock, Saetta asked to speak to Warden Lawes. It was of vital importance, he said—a matter of life and death. He told the warden that Mrs. Antonio was innocent; that he (Saetta) and Faraci were solely to blame. When apprised of the condemned man's statement, the governor postponed the execution. The woman, who had been waiting to be summoned, fainted on hearing the news. From then on, she felt confident that she would never see the other side of that door through which the condemned pass, never to return.

I went back to the prison the next night, there to learn that a week's reprieve had been granted. Another respite followed for the consideration of new evidence. Mrs. Antonio and her hired accomplices were given until August 9 to live. I expected that she would finally receive a commutation of sentence.

On the night of the execution, a friend drove me to Sing Sing. There was considerable excitement at the main entrance, so I obtained permission to take the car in by another gate. I mention this seemingly unimportant fact because it was to cause me some difficulty before the night was over.

There was speculation in the death chamber as to how the condemned woman would be at the end. She had been hysterical and in a semicoma much of the day, and had remarked that she would not be able to walk to her doom. The doctors were of the opinion that she would collapse when the time came.

Within a few minutes of the fatal hour, Mrs. Antonio sent for Warden Lawes. To him, she said:

"I don't care what you do to me. I'm not afraid to die. I have nothing on my conscience because I never killed anyone. There was always plenty of dope and guns in the house, and I could have killed my husband any time I wanted."

Then she declared that one of the two men who were to be executed with her had informed her that he intended to murder her husband. She told him, she said, that it did not matter, for her only interest was in the children.

Mrs. Antonio was on her knees in prayer when the acting principal keeper called for her. She was attired in a dress which she had made during her imprisonment. It was a pretty garment-blue with bits of white trimming on the sleeves and across the front.

As she stepped from her cell, guards started to carry her; but she indicated that she would not need any assistance. Unfalteringly, she walked the entire distance to the chair. Approaching from the back to affix the head electrode, I could see that she was extremely nervous. Her voice trembled as she repeated the prayer with Father McCaffrey. A wave of pity for this frail little mother swept over me.

After my night's work was done, I left the death house. At the gate through which my friend and I had entered the prison, we were stopped. The guard demanded to know who we were. Although I explained, we still were not allowed to pass. He had not been on duty when we came in, and eyed us with suspicion. He notified his superior, and search began for an official who had authority to order our release.

While this was going on, the two of us had visions of spending the rest of the night within the grim walls of Sing Sing. I knew that my failure to arrive home would worry Mrs. Elliott. Fortunately, the proper officer was found, but even then the car was thoroughly searched before we were permitted to leave.

The cases of Mrs. Creighton and Mrs. Antonio prove the need for segregation of those under sentence of death. It has always been my belief that if we are to have capital punishment, we should provide institutions for that purpose entirely apart from other prisons. Moreover, the buildings should be so constructed that the condemned person awaiting his turn would not have to suffer unnecessary torture when others go to their deaths. He could be kept in ignorance of these executions and the distressing details attending them.

Under present conditions, the knowledge that a man or a woman is about to be put to death frequently breeds unrest among the other prisoners, and makes them ugly. It can have a devastating effect on the convict who is serving time for a minor crime, and is in prison supposedly for reclamation by society. In the case of the hardened, desperate criminal who is antisocial, the unrest born of an execution can have, and often has had, serious consequences. Separate places for the condemned would prevent such an undesirable situation.

One of the most popular inmates of Sing Sing's death house was Eva Coo. She had been found guilty of plotting and helping in the murder of her handyman, Gimpy Harry Wright, to collect the $12,000 insurance which she had taken out on him. The conviction was obtained largely on the testimony of Mrs. Martha Clift, who also was involved in the crime. Mrs. Clift escaped with a prison term by supplying the evidence that placed Eva in the chair. According to the prosecution, Eva struck Wright on the head with a claw hammer, and then instructed the other woman to run over him with an automobile.

Throughout her imprisonment, Eva remained good-natured and cheerful. She had a pleasant word for everybody. Consequently, she was liked by those who came in contact with her, and they hoped that executive clemency would be exercised in her behalf.

The woman's only complaint was about her physical condition. She frequently suffered painful headaches, doubtless brought on by her plight. But even these did not dampen her spirits or affect her disposition.

When I arrived at Sing Sing on the night of June 27, 1935, the date of Mrs. Coo's execution, gloom was everywhere I went. In the administration building and in the death chamber, the talk was all of Eva. Nearly everyone I met was hopeful that the governor would intervene. However, he would have to act soon if the execution were to be halted.

Shortly before eleven o'clock, Warden Lawes visited Mrs. Coo in her cell. She stood up to greet him. A matron rolled down one of Eva's stockings for the leg electrode. Addressing the warden, the condemned woman said:

"In two minutes, I'm going to die. I know nothing can save me. Before God, I'm innocent of this. Honest, Warden."

On the way to the execution chamber, Mrs. Coo called out to Leonard Scarnici, who was to follow her to the chair in a few minutes for the killing of a detective.

"So long, Len," she said.

"So long, Eva," he shouted back. "Keep your chin up, kid."

"I will," she assured him.

And she did. She appeared resigned to her fate as she walked to the chair. For a second, she watched me soaking the head electrode, and then sat down. Guards quickly strapped her in.

"Good-by, darlings," she said to the matrons, who stood in front of her. Her words were not intended to be flippant. They were earnestly spoken.

I could feel Eva shudder as I affixed the headpiece. When the mask was placed over her face, she gasped, "Oh!"

The most courageous person I have ever seen on the edge of eternity was a woman. Her name was Irene Schroeder, and she was only twenty-two. I believe she knew no fear.

Irene Schroeder became on February 23, 1931, the first woman to die in Pennsylvania's electric chair. With Glenn Dague, the salesman and Sunday school teacher who had deserted his family in a little West Virginia town to go with her, she was executed for the murder of Corporal Brady Paul, a state policeman.

Prior to the slaying of the officer, the pair had committed a series of petty crimes. It was while they were fleeing from a grocery store robbery in Butler, Pennsylvania, that Corporal Paul and Private Ernest Moore, of the highway patrol, attempted to apprehend them. Irene fatally shot Paul, and the other trooper was wounded. In the car at the time was her four-year-old son, Donnie.

Leaving the boy with relatives in West Virginia, Irene and Dague dashed across the country, hunted by the law. Cornered in Arizona, they fought it out with posse, were captured after their ammunition gave out, and were returned to Pennsylvania for trial. Donnie's innocent remark to a detective that "my mother killed a cop like you" aided the state in getting a conviction.

Irene was a model prisoner while awaiting the walk to the chair. She was always agreeable and considerate. She never found fault with anything, and caused her attendants no trouble. Little wonder that the matrons grew so fond of her.

Love is a word carelessly used in the accounts of crime; but I firmly believe that Irene Schroeder loved Glenn Dague with full and unfaltering devotion. She proved this at the trial and during her subsequent imprisonment. She was perfectly willing to shoulder the entire responsibility if Dague's life would be spared. On the motor trip to Rockview Penitentiary for execution, the two constantly caressed each other.

The condemned woman slept comparatively well the night before her death. When a matron awakened her the next day, she asked Irene: "How are you this morning?"

"Fine," Irene replied calmly.

"Can I do anything for you?" the matron wanted to know.

Irene shook her head—then quickly changed her mind.

"Yes, there is something," she said. "Please tell them in the kitchen to fry Glenn's eggs on both sides. He likes them that way."

I had reached Bellefonte on the preceding day. Instead of going to a hotel as I usually do, I stayed with a friend. This was to avoid reporters and photographers, who seemed to be everywhere. An officer picked me up early the next morning, and drove me to the prison.

Across the entrance to the grounds stood a car containing two state policemen. We were stopped, but were permitted to pass after convincing the men of our identity. Troopers were stationed all around the penitentiary. This precaution proved unnecessary, for the early-morning hour and the location of the prison kept the curious away.

Without delay, I went directly to the execution room, and made certain that everything was in readiness. A

154

guard informed me that the woman would present no difficulty. "She's a game one," he remarked.

To the prison chaplain who appeared at her cell to accompany her to the death chamber, Irene said quietly: "Don't worry about me. I'll be all right. You'd better go back to Glenn. I think he needs you more than I do." She probably realized that she was the stronger of the two then as she had been in their crime-spotted life together when she had dominated him. Now, in recompense, she was anxious to assume whatever part of his burden she could.

Clad in a loose and poorly fitting gray dress, Irene was brought into the execution room at precisely seven A.M. The clergyman preceded her, having refused to eave her side because another spiritual adviser was with Dague. The minister was repeating the Twenty-third Psalm as the procession entered the chamber.

I watched Irene as she walked to the chair, a guard on each side of her. There was a smile on her face—the most pleasant I have seen on anyone. It was not a smile of defiance or of bravado, but a kindly, peaceful one.

With a certain dignity, she sat down. She seemed willing to pay her debt to the state. Perhaps she felt that without Dague there could be no life for her. While the straps and electrodes were being adjusted, she glanced at the witnesses, then closed her eyes. Two and a half minutes later, the prison physician pronounced her dead.

Newspapers had called her "Iron Irene" and "The Tiger Girl." Those terms may have applied during her association with Dague. But as she played her role in the grim scene of the death chamber, there was something stronger, yet softer, than iron to make her the most composed and fearless person I have ever put to death. I emerged from the prison that morning feeling something akin to admiration for Irene Schroeder.

I have often been asked whether there is any difference in the methods of executing a man and a woman. There is none whatever. The procedure is exactly the same. However, I am probably more deliberate in the

155

case of a woman. By that, I do not mean I am slower, but simply more painstaking in my efforts to avoid a mishap of any kind.

SIX IN ONE DAY

January 6, 1927, was my busiest day as society's agent of death. Within twenty-four hours, I executed six men—three for the State of Massachusetts and the same number for the State of New York.

There was a striking similarity between these two multiple executions. In each instance, the three prisoners gave up their lives for the murder of one man. Both crimes were alike, also, in that an elderly watchman had been killed during the commission of a robbery.

Early on the morning of January 5, I left my home for Boston, arriving there about one P.M. After registering at a hotel and telephoning the warden of the state prison at Charlestown, I went to a motion picture show. The feature was a light, sparkling comedy, and helped me to forget the task which lay ahead of me.

By the time I reached the prison that night, a crowd of more than fifteen hundred had jammed the square in front of the main gate. The case had attracted considerable attention throughout Massachusetts. All of the three men scheduled to die—John J. Devereaux, John J. McLaughlin, and Edward H. Heinlein—were young, the oldest being thirty. Armed with revolvers and wearing handkerchiefs over their faces, the trio, together with two others, had held up the Waltham car barns of the Middlesex and Boston Street Railway Company in October, 1925, and stolen in the neighborhood of $1,500. During the robbery, Devereaux shot James H. Furneau, the sixty-seven-year-old watchman, in the leg, and beat him on the head with the pistol butt. The man died as the result of his injuries.

Several days passed before an arrest. Then, acting on a mysterious tip, the authorities picked up the quintet, and charged them with the crime. At the trial, Devereaux readily admitted the shooting, but claimed self-defense. First-degree murder verdicts were returned against three of the defendants.

Efforts to save the young thugs from the chair started immediately. Appeals were filed, and there was a state-wide campaign to persuade Governor Fuller to commute the sentences to life imprisonment. Two reprieves were obtained from the governor. On the day that one of these was granted, I had gone to Boston for the execution, only to learn of the stay. Almost up to the time that the men walked to the chair on January 6, frantic pleas for executive clemency or court intervention continued.

The executions, which began at 12:03 A.M., were without unusual incident. All three men bore up bravely, not once faltering as they walked to their deaths. Heinlein, who occupied the cell nearest the death chamber, was the first to go. He repeated the prayers after his spiritual adviser until I threw the switch. Next was Devereaux. Though pale, he was composed, and also recited the prayers. McLaughlin, not as calm as the others, was last, and he prayed fervently, his voice filling the entire room. At one point, he missed the words of the priest. "I can't hear you, Father," he said. The clergyman nodded, and repeated the words.

Warden Hendry was very much impressed by the trio's fortitude, and mentioned this fact to me afterward. He also spoke of the quickness and humaneness with which the routine was carried out. In the case of one of the men, only fifty-eight seconds had elapsed between the time he stepped into the death chamber and the instant the current was turned on.

158

Upon leaving the prison, I went directly to my hotel, where I slept for several hours. Then I took a train for New York City. Mrs. Elliott, Frances, and a doctor (a friend of mine) met me at the station. The physician was going along to Sing Sing that night to witness the executions there.

As I had several free hours, we decided to attend a movie. The doctor suggested a Broadway theater where he was acquainted with the manager. At the theater, I found that the feature was the same one I had seen in Boston the previous afternoon. However, my wife and daughter were anxious to see it, so the doctor and I chatted with the manager in his office during the show.

At first, the talk was of trivial things; but eventually it got around to my work for the state. It always does when I am with strangers. The manager mentioned the fact that he had witnessed a hanging some years before. The circumstances were most unusual, he said. Pressed for details, he related an amazing story.

In his younger days, he had been manager of a stock company that toured the country. While in Texas, the troupe played a certain town for more than a week. The sheriff attended nearly every performance, and applauded loudly. On the last night, he visited backstage.

"Say, that's a great show you got," he complimented the manager. "Best I've ever seen, and I ain't missed a one that's been' here." Then he whispered: "Drop down to the jail tomorrow morning and see me. I've got a little surprise for you."

Somewhat mystified, the manager called at the sheriff's office about nine o'clock the next morning. He was treated royally, being escorted around the premises and allowed to talk with the prisoners. During the tour of inspection, the sheriff announced:

"Something special's going to happen here today. We're going to hang at noon. That's why I wanted you to come down."

The actor was astonished. He had not heard of the case, and knew nothing of the impending execution. Finally, he said:

"It was mighty nice of you to think of me, Sheriff; but I'm afraid I won't be able to see it. We're leaving on the 11:45 train. I'm to meet the troupe at the railroad station."

"Oh, pshaw!" exclaimed the disappointed sheriff. "Sure you can't stay?"

"Positive."

The sheriff became thoughtful. "What time do you have to get away from here to catch that train?" he asked.

"About 11:15," the manager answered.

The sheriff took out his watch. It was then ten o' clock. He summoned an attendant.

"Go in and tell Sam I'm setting the clock ahead an hour," he ordered. "Tell him to eat his dinner, and be ready at eleven o'clock."

Turning to the manager, the sheriff beamed:

"There, how's that? Now you can see him swing."

"You shouldn't have done that," the manager said.

"And why not?" demanded the sheriff. "What's an hour more or less to a fellow who's going to be killed. He's got to be hung, so you might as well see it."

Obviously, the sheriff thought he had done his newly found friend a great favor. The latter was not so sure.

Precisely at eleven o'clock, the man was taken from his cell and hanged. In the fall through the trap, his neck did not break, and he kicked his legs free from their bonds. He groaned as he slowly strangled to death. It was a horrifying sight, especially for a person who had never witnessed an execution before. It was one that the theater manager will never forget.

After the motion picture show was over, the doctor and I took Mrs. Elliott and Frances to the train. Then we had dinner and started for Sing Sing. Though three men were to be put to death, there was little excitement at the prison. In fact, one would hardly have known it was an execution night.

Those to die were Charles Golden, Edgar Humes, and George Williams. About a year before, they had slain William M. Young, a watchman, during the robbery of a Manhattan silk loft. A jury speedily doomed them.

"One of the boys almost cheated the chair this afternoon," a death house guard informed me while I was making final preparations.

"How come?" I asked.

"He was going to commit suicide, but his little scheme didn't work. We caught him just in time."

The guard explained that an attendant had noticed a bulge under Williams' shirt. Investigation disclosed that the condemned man had tied four towels together in an improvised rope, and was trying to conceal it. It was assumed that he had intended to thwart justice by ending his own life before it could be claimed by the state. The towels were taken away from him, and he was kept under constant surveillance until he walked "the last mile."

When their turns came, each of the men shuffled stolidly into the death chamber. The order was Golden, Humes, and Williams. None spoke or displayed any emotion. The Catholic chaplain accompanied two of them, the Protestant chaplain the other.

Following the execution, Benjamin Bradley, another man who also was convicted of participation in the same murder, sought all the details. He wanted to know how his pals had acted when face to face with death. A guard told him, after which Bradley said, "Thanks, boss. Ah hopes Ah'll be as brave." He went to the chair a week later.

My busiest day as executioner over, I returned home. The fact that I had sent six men into eternity within a little less than twenty-four hours apparently affected me no more than if there had been only one.

While multiple executions may be more trying for the warden and the death house attendants, they present no particular problem for me. I found this out in 1926 when I was called upon to execute three men in a single night. Of course, on such occasions, I always arrange to have a sufficient number of electrodes on hand, as well as effective means of cooling them off.

Since taking over the work, I have officiated at a number of group executions. Eight times I have been the agent of death for a state which demanded that four men give up their lives on the same day. Thirty times the chair's toll has been three, and on fifty-three occasions I have electrocuted two people within a few minutes.

Multiple executions invariably increase the requests for appointments as witnesses. This is partly because so-called mass executions are given wide publicity, and partly because there are morbid individuals who would prefer to see more than one person die. As a spectator explained it, "the more there are, the better the show."

Frankly, it has always been a mystery to me why people voluntarily attend executions. Yet I know that many clamor for admittance to the death chamber every time somebody pays the extreme penalty. Sing Sing alone has a waiting list of more than a thousand would-be spectators.

Witnesses other than prison officials are usually nec-essary under the law. Their presence is required so they can verify that the mandate of the court was properly carried out. After the execution, they must sign a document certifying that they saw put to death the person whose name appears thereon.

The number of witnesses varies in different states. For instance, New York must have twelve. Pennsylvania requires six, in addition to whom there may be half a dozen newspaper reporters. Massachusetts keeps its executions more exclusive, allowing only three outside spectators, who are always representatives of the leading wire services.

Although the law stipulates what officials and how many witnesses must watch society avenged, it fails, in most states, to limit the number. The capacity of the death chamber does that. I have seen more than seventy-five crowded into the stuffy room. To satisfy as many applicants as possible, witnesses were changed one night after the first two men had died at a quadruple execution in New Jersey.

Selecting the official guests rests with the warden. Frequently, it is no easy task, especially if the case is a celebrated one. Newspapers want to cover the story so they can describe the lurid details to their readers; professional men desire to observe what happens from a medical or scientific standpoint; thrill-seekers are anxious for a new and more exciting experience.

Connecticut allows the condemned person to have a hand in picking those who are to see him sent into eternity. The prisoner may choose three spectators, if he so desires. They must, however, be adult males.

Invitations to executions are usually mailed out several days ahead of time. Sing Sing employs a printed form on which names and dates are filled in with a typewriter. It reads as follows:

Dear Sir:

In accordance with Section 507 of the Code of Criminal Procedure you are hereby invited to be present as a witness at the execution by electricity of (*Name*) which will occur at this prison on (*Date*).

The hour of 11 P.M. has been designated by me for such execution and you will arrange to be at my office in this prison not later than 10 o'clock P.M.

I would thank you to treat this communication as confidential and advise me immediately upon its receipt of your acceptance or otherwise, so that I can make arrangements accordingly.

Under no circumstances is this invitation transferable.

Very respectfully,

LEWIS E. LAWES

Warden.

People from all walks of life eagerly seek such invitations. Oddly enough, the majority are professional people—doctors, lawyers, writers, engineers, and the like. A surprisingly large number of requests come from clergymen. Occasionally, those associated with the arrest or trial of the prisoner ask for passes.

Weeks before an execution, applications for admittance pour in on the prison authorities. I am sometimes annoyed for days. Appeals are also made to public officials and politicians—even the governor. If these efforts fail, there are individuals who go to the prison in the hope of being called in at the last minute. I have been stopped at the entrance several times by those who were anxious to act as witnesses. One night three New York City policemen who had driven to Sing Sing urged me to use my influence to get them into the death chamber when the state took the lives of three men who had killed a detective they knew. I refused, of course.

I heard a story not long ago about a rich playboy who sat next to a warden at a banquet. In the course of the dinner, the young man expressed a desire to see "a dirty rat burn in the hot seat." He added that he would be glad to pay the prison head a thousand dollars for the privilege. The indignant warden had all he could do to contain himself.

Some people, such as physicians and newspaper reporters, have good reason for attending executions. Others, for the most part, are morbidly curious, and find it necessary to advance all kinds of weak explanations for wanting to participate in the grim business. Any warden's mail prior to an execution furnishes abundant evidence of this.

A foe of capital punishment is convinced that he could more effectively aid the cause if he might observe what takes place in the death chamber. A legislator who is seriously considering the introduction of a bill to abolish the death penalty in his state wants to view at least one execution before acting. A clergyman has always desired to know how a murderer behaves on the brink of eternity. A scientist is anxious to determine whether the chair is more humane than other forms of execution. A dentist would like to find out what effect, if any, electric current has on the teeth. And so the letters run.

Friends or relatives of both the murdered person and the condemned sometimes ask for permission to be in the room when death is meted out. Although rare, there have been instances when such requests have been granted. In Pennsylvania, a father watched his son's killer go to the chair. Before the execution, he came to my hotel in Bellefonte, and talked with me for several hours. After describing how his son had been slain, he said bitterly, "I wish they'd let me throw the switch on that fellow." I was afraid he might be demonstrative in the' death chamber, but he was quiet and emotionless as the prisoner was led to his doom.

A year or so later, another man was present when his wife's murderer was electrocuted. He, too, would have liked to substitute for me at that time. He was sorry, he told me, that the execution was so quick and so humane. It should have been slow and torturous, he declared.

I have never approved of relatives of the murdered victim serving as witnesses. As I have pointed out before, I have always felt that if the judgment of the court is carried out in capital cases, vengeance should play no part in the matter.

Inflicting punishment by death has its peculiar fascination for women as well as men. Most wardens, however, will not invite female witnesses. Their irrevocable decision is based on the fact that women, as a rule, cannot stand up under the strain. Only once in my experience have women who were not prison matrons been in the death chamber during an execution. This was in New Jersey, and there were two present on that occasion.

Witnesses to executions are usually searched for articles which must not be taken into the death chamber. Upon entering the room, they sometimes shove one another for positions of vantage. If there for the first time, they observe every detail of their surroundings. When the condemned is brought in, all eyes are on him. Ears are strained to catch his last words, should he speak.

Those who gaze upon a man or woman in the electric chair react in different ways. I have seen them turn pale, tremble, or gag as they watched life depart from a human being. I have seen them stare off into space; cover their

165

eyes with their hands or with handkerchiefs; fidget nervously with some piece of clothing. I have heard them groan feebly or cry out. On a night that four boys went to the chair, a witness fainted, and had to be removed from the room. But the great majority of the spectators are calm and orderly.

As if looking on while a life was being snuffed out were not enough, some try to peek into or enter the autopsy room after it is all over. Officers have actually had to order a few to leave with the others, so insistent were they on remaining.

For most volunteer witnesses, one execution is plenty. However, there are those who return as often as they can obtain invitations. I recall a man who attended a number of executions. He probably would have continued if he had not had a rather unpleasant experience at one of them. On this particular night, he sat in the front row. As a man who had just been lifted from the chair was wheeled past him, the dead man's hand accidentally fell on the witness' lap. He jerked back in horror. I never saw him in the death chamber again.

There was a night at Sing Sing when six were scheduled to die in the chair. The sentences of four were finally commuted, but executive clemency was not extended to the two ringleaders. A friend of mine who had received an invitation drove to the prison with me. While in the visitors' room awaiting the summons to the warden's office, he engaged in conversation with another witness.

"Your first execution?" he was asked.

My friend nodded.

"It's my second," said the other witness. "I was up here about a year ago, and saw two of them go. I didn't have any trouble getting in to the first one, but it was different this time. Guess it's more difficult when there's a mass execution."

"I'd hardly call this a mass execution," my friend commented.

The other man looked puzzled. "If half a dozen killings in one night aren't a mass execution, then I don't know one."

It was quite evident that he was totally ignorant of the fact that the governor had spared the lives of four. My friend broke the news to him.

"Well, that's a fine mess," he sputtered. "Here I come all the way up from New York [a train ride of about an hour] to see six get the works, and a chickenhearted governor lets four of them off. If I'd ever dreamed he'd pull a stunt like that, I'd have stayed home."

He raved on:

"And would you believe it, I voted twice for that fellow. But I'll never do it again—never! Any man who lets murderers off as easy as that will never get another vote of mine. It's an outrage. Something ought to be done about it."

I, too, feel that something should be done about it— something that would bar that kind of man from being the wide-eyed, morbid witness as a fellow human is put to death by the authority of the state in which he and too many others like him may vote.

WERE THEY INNOCENT?

I have often wondered whether I have ever executed an innocent person. Such a thought has flashed through my mind as I have heard a condemned prisoner, standing before or sitting in the electric chair, emphatically declare that he did not commit the crime for which he was about to forfeit his life.

This has happened not once or twice, but many times in my experience. More than thirty people whom I have put to death protested their innocence to the very end. Some swore before their Maker or on the names of their mothers that they were guiltless. Others called upon the Almighty to attest to the truth of their dying statements.

Nothing in the death chamber disturbs me more than to hear a person with only a few seconds to live insist that justice has erred. When this occurs, my steps from the chair to the controls are slower than usual. My hand seems to hesitate on the switch. Greater effort is necessary to perform the execution.

I shall never forget the morning of November 21, 1927, when a man was brought to the chair in Rockview Penitentiary. His name was Jerry Weeks, and he had been convicted of murder on circumstantial evidence.

Throughout his trial and imprisonment, Weeks had been practically friendless. But there was one man, a Salvation Army chaplain, who was interested in the

168

doomed man. He visited Weeks a number of times, and finally came to the conclusion that he was innocent. Consequently, the case worried him a great deal. On the morning of the execution, the chaplain sought permission to question Weeks after he had been placed in the chair. This was an unusual request especially in Pennsylvania, where death-chamber speeches by the condemned are not permitted. However, the religious man was so earnest and so much respected for his work in the prison that his wish was granted.

Weeks walked to the chair with a firm step, sat down, and was strapped in. Not a word passed his lips. That he was resigned to his fate was apparent. Before the electrodes were applied, the Salvation Army man, who had accompanied him into the execution room, stepped to the chair and looked into his face.

"Jerry," he said quietly, "you have only a few more seconds of this life to live. What you say now cannot help you. No earthly power can save you. I have been your friend, and believe in you. With your last breath, I want you to tell me the truth. Are you guilty of this murder for which you are going to die?"

"You're the only friend I got," he answered. "I wouldn't lie to you. In the name of my mother in heaven, I'm innocent."

The chaplain bowed his head, and backed away from the chair. I thought I detected tears in his eyes. The electrodes were quickly adjusted, the mask was put over the man's face, and my hand, not wholly steady, threw the switch.

On the train a few hours later, I had an opportunity to talk with the Salvation Army chaplain. We discussed Weeks' case at some length and also what had transpired in the death chamber.

"You were alone with him many times," I said, "and he doubtless told you things he didn't tell anybody else. Do you really believe he was innocent?"

"I'm convinced of it," he replied.

In my record book, I wrote that night: "This is a case in which circumstantial evidence could be wrong."

Just three days before Weeks' execution, I had had a rather harrowing experience. I had sent four men into eternity for the State of New Jersey. They were "Big Joe" and "Little Joe" Juliano, Christopher Barone, and Louis Capozzi. The prosecution had proved to the satisfaction of the courts that the quartet had killed a man in an ice cream company payroll robbery in Newark.

The first to go was "Big Joe" Juliano, who was accompanied into the death chamber by two clergymen. Before the doomed man took his seat, the principal keeper invited him to speak. "Big Joe" had expected this, and had planned what to say. Glaring at the seventy-five witnesses who crowded the stuffy chamber, he cried:

"I was framed up, and not only by the police. I'm innocent as God Almighty. I swear it on my holy mother's honor. They're murdering me like a dog. I'm innocent as God Almighty. I'm innocent, I tell you."

Guards gently pushed him into the chair, where he continued to affirm his innocence. As my hand reached for the switch, he shouted again: "They're murdering me like a dog! Good-by! Let 'er go!"

Barone had hardly set foot into the room before he said: "Gentlemen, I'm innocent as God. Captain Brex [Newark police officer] caused you to kill me. Don't forget to take care of my mother."

He then kissed the priest. "Good-by, Father. God bless you."

His last words, screamed from the chair, were: "I'm innocent as God Almighty, I tell you!"

Next was "Little Joe" Juliano, cousin of the first man. He also spoke, but not as excitedly as the two who had preceded him. "Gentlemen," he begged, "I want to ask the men who committed the crime for which I'm to die to come forward on their dying beds, confess, and clear my name."

Handing his crucifix to a priest who was there at his request, he said, "Give this to my wife, Father." The priest nodded, and the condemned man kissed him.

But "Little Joe" had not finished. He had more to say. "I couldn't die with a lie on my lips, gentlemen," he declared after he had been strapped in the chair. "I'm innocent. Good-by." He was praying when the current struck him.

Similar avowals poured from the lips of Capozzi. "I'm as innocent as God Himself," he told those in the room. "The police framed me." After kissing the crucifix and asking the priest to give it to his sister, he continued:

"Gentlemen, I die with a smile on my lips. I'm an innocent man."

Then he called a farewell to his attorney. The current choked a prayer he had started.

Returning home that night, I thought of what these men had said. I considered it odd that their statements had been so much alike. It was as though they had conferred among themselves, and decided on exactly what they would say.

Bad as this quadruple execution was, it did not affect me so much as one at Sing Sing Prison on a sultry night in July, 1930. At that time, three men—Stephen Grezchowiak, Max Rybarczyk, and Alexander Bogdanoff—paid the supreme penalty for the slaying and robbing of a Buffalo restaurant owner.

Grezchowiak, the lead-off man, entered the execution chamber smoking a cigarette. He asked permission to finish it, and was allowed to do so. After dropping the butt on the floor and sitting down in the chair, he addressed the witnesses.

"I hope the citizens of Buffalo are satisfied at sending an innocent man to the chair," he said.

He stopped for a second or two as a guard stood in front of him to adjust the strap, then, continued, his voice rising:

"Take a good look, gentlemen. Keep your eyes open. You are seeing an innocent man die."

The second to go that night was Rybarczyk. He was nervous as we prepared him for the end. When a guard was about to put the mask over his face, he spoke. "Well,

171

gentlemen, I'm an innocent man. I'm going to leave you in a minute."

Bogdanoff supplied the dramatic climax. He took a position directly in front of the chair, and raised his right arm for attention—a totally unnecessary gesture, for all eyes were riveted on him.

"Gentlemen," he declared slowly and deliberately, "you represent the State of New York. You have just seen the state kill two innocent men. I tried to prevent it, but my word was no good. Now, as I stand before this funny-looking piece of furniture, I swear before God they were innocent."

His speech finished, he sat down in the "funny-looking piece of furniture," and attendants strapped him fast. While this was going on, the priest was intoning the prayers. Bogdanoff listened for a few seconds, and then interrupted sharply: "Why pray for me? I don't give a damn."

As I threw the switch to end another human life, his last words burned into my brain. I wondered whether he had spoken the truth, whether I actually had executed two innocent people. It was a terrible, soul-shrinking thought.

Perhaps the calmest protestation of innocence I have ever heard was uttered by Everett C. Applegate, who, with Mrs. Mary Frances Creighton, had been convicted of the poison-death of his wife. Long before he became enmeshed in a chain of circumstances which led to murder, he had been a soldier. On the night of his execution, he died like one.

Applegate fairly rushed to the chair, and upon reaching it, turned and faced the witnesses. He drew himself erect, and spoke in a steady, clear voice. There was not the slightest trace of a quaver.

"Gentlemen," he said, "before I am to die, I wish to say something." He hesitated for a second to make sure there was no objection, and went on:

"Before God and man, I am absolutely innocent of this crime. May God have mercy on the soul of Martin W.

Littleton." Littleton was the district attorney who had prosecuted the case.

As I regulated the current, a question kept repeating itself in my mind. How could a person on the brink of eternity swear before his Maker that he was guiltless unless he was telling the truth? I did not attempt to answer it then, but I have pondered it many times since.

Another who acted in a similar manner was Edward Metelski. Early in his career of crime, he had been warned by a New Jersey state trooper that he would some day "wind up in the chair." To this, he laughingly retorted, "If I ever do, come and see me off." Five years later, the trooper was present when Metelski was electrocuted at Trenton for the killing of a state policeman.

Strapped in the chair, Metelski asked to speak, but did not wait for an answer. He said: "You people are watching an innocent man being murdered. I hope God forgives you for this. I hope He forgives me for all the things I've done wrong."

Alexander Kasprzcak was convicted of doing away with his uncle for the purpose of collecting insurance. He, also, insisted that the taking of his life was a miscarriage of justice. "I'm innocent," he declared. "I've got a wife and five children. I die in this chair innocently. God bless everybody here."

There was no such humility in the heart of Louis Lazar when he went to his death—only hatred, especially for the daughter of the man he had been found guilty of murdering. The hired killer, as the police called him, talked hurriedly as he stood in front of the chair. He had several things he wished to point out, and was afraid the officers in the execution chamber would not let him finish.

"I want to say, gentlemen," he began, "that a maid said the man she saw on the stairs—the murderer—had dark, wavy hair, and was five feet, five inches tall. Saskowitz's daughter said she saw him, too. Well, I'm only five feet two, and my hair isn't like that, is it?"

He hastened on:

"But Saskowitz's daughter wouldn't testify for me. If there is another world where I'm going now, I hope I'll be the star witness when she goes up. That's all I want to say, gentlemen. Thank you."

In Massachusetts one night in 1929, a man was brought to the chair for the slaying of a girl. The verdict on which the state had demanded the supreme penalty had been based on circumstantial evidence. Yet no link seemed to be missing. Prior to the execution, the father of the murdered girl appealed to the governor to save the prisoner from the chair. His plea was to no avail, however, and the man went to his doom—but not before he had sent a letter of appreciation to that father.

"I thank you for what you have done for me," the condemned man wrote. "I never saw your dear daughter in my life, and I want to say to you that I am not guilty, and that every word I said at my trial was the very truth."

All of these cases were, of course, reviewed by the courts. They also were carefully weighed by the governor or the Board of Pardons hearing the applications for clemency. Nothing could be found to warrant a reversal of the verdicts or the lessening of the degree of punishment. These people, it was decided, were guilty "beyond a reasonable doubt," and should pay with their lives.

Yet, in spite of conclusive evidence against them—in several instances, their own confessions—these men protested their innocence to the very end. This may seem strange to many, as it has to me. However, various explanations may be offered.

Some whom I have executed were not murderers.

That is, they did not actually kill anyone. They may not have been in possession of a deadly weapon when the slaying occurred, or even have been on the scene of the crime. But they were either a part of the conspiracy or involved in the commission of a felony which resulted in a death. In the eyes of the law, they were as guilty of murder as the one who really committed it. It is easy to understand, then, why these people went to the chair with the feeling that they were dying for something they did not do.

A good example of this was the case of the four men who were put to death in Pennsylvania in 1927 for the slaying of a policeman. The fatal bullet was fired while three of the group were being pursued for an attempted bank robbery. The fourth member of the gang had fled to another section of the city, and was arrested about fifteen minutes before the officer was shot. He could not possibly have had a hand in the killing. But he had participated in an illegal enterprise which ended in murder. Consequently, he was convicted and executed with the others.

Consideration for loved ones and friends has doubtless prompted a number of the condemned to die with a declaration of innocence. They wanted those who had faith in them to retain that faith. Or they may have thought that by their last words they lessened the pain of those upon whom they had brought suffering and disgrace. I know of at least one such instance.

A young man of twenty-one killed a storekeeper who had interrupted his rifling of a cash register. There was no question as to the youth's guilt. Witnesses heard the shot, and saw him running from the store. In fact, he himself admitted the crime shortly after his arrest. However, his mother could not bring herself to believe that her son was a murderer. When anyone pointed to his confession, she would reply, "The police forced him to sign it."

"Mom thinks I didn't do it," the condemned youth told a guard on the day of his execution. "It would hurt her terribly if she thought I did. I've got to make her go on believing I didn't do it. Besides, there's my sister and brothers to think about. It would be pretty tough on them to have a murderer in the family."

That night he walked to the chair without any outward sign of emotion. As he was being strapped in, he said: "I'm innocent. God bless my mother. Good-by."

Inmates of the death house have a great deal of time in which to think. Perhaps that is why some are able to

175

justify their misdeeds in their own minds, or excuse themselves by placing the blame on a weakness or a subversive influence.

"The dirty rat had it coming to him," raved one gangster in his cell. "They ought to thank me, not kill me, for plugging him." This man, oddly enough, died repeating the word "innocent."

A boy from the slums of New York's East Side attributed his downfall to his environment. Society, he maintained, was responsible for what had happened. "I never had a chance," he wailed. "Now because I made a mistake, they're going to take me out and kill me." The "mistake" was the fatal shooting of a policeman.

Drink is often held as the cause of the condemned's plight, and ordinarily those who were intoxicated when they murdered cannot seem to comprehend why they should go to the chair. "I didn't know what I was doing," is the plea in most cases. Chester White, a man who had killed a woman and her fifteen-year-old daughter in a drunken frenzy, claimed that he "saw shadows."

A psychiatrist once told me that murderers who confessed their guilt have been known to convince themselves, during their long wait in the death house that they had not killed. As a consequence, they have, gone to the chair wildly protesting, and actually believing in, their innocence.

How would I feel if I were to learn that I had executed an innocent person? Words could hardly describe my reaction. But I must add in all frankness that I would not consider the responsibility mine, except as that of a member of a society that demands a life for a life. I would not have sat in judgment on this unfortunate creature. Neither would I have decreed that he should die. A court would have done that. My only responsibility would have been to carry out the order of the court as humanely as possible.

UNFORGETTABLE MOMENTS

I have had several harrowing experiences in the death chamber, but there was one in particular that cut deep into my memory. It gave me the most spine-chilling moment I have ever known.

On a Friday night a few years after I had taken up the work of executioner, Mrs. Elliott and I went to see a motion picture at our neighborhood theater. Although we deliberately try to avoid films dealing with crime and penal institutions, we unknowingly run into one now and then. This is what happened that night.

There was nothing in the title to suggest that the picture was of crime and punishment–capital punishment. The story was about a young man who, driven by an overpowering love for a girl, assumed responsibility for a murder he had not committed. On what seemed to be an incontrovertible skein of circumstantial evidence, he was convicted, and subsequently sentenced to die in the electric chair.

A minute or two after the youth had been electrocuted, the governor telephoned the warden that he was granting a reprieve for the consideration of new evidence. The person who was really guilty had confessed. But it was, of course, too late. The man was dead. The state had executed an innocent person.

It was a powerful bit of acting, and, I am frank to admit, it made a lasting impression on me. My wife and I talked about it on the way home.

"Such a thing could happen in real life," I said as I hurriedly recalled some of the executions I had performed in which the verdict had been reached on circumstantial evidence. "It's highly improbable, but it could happen. I hope and pray that if it ever does, I won't be the man who threw the switch." Mrs. Elliott felt the same way.

The following Monday found me at Rockview Penitentiary, where a single execution was scheduled for seven o'clock that morning. I had not read of the case, and did not even know the condemned man's name until I arrived at the prison. While I was making my usual inquiries, an officer remarked:

"This fellow's like most of them. He swears he didn't have anything to do with the murder, and has been saying so ever since he got here."

When the prisoner was brought into the execution room at the appointed hour, preceded by a clergyman of his faith, I observed that he was a comparatively clean-cut youth. It was obvious that he had spent a cruelly wakeful night, thinking only of what awaited him in the morning. But he was resolute, and, though fear was plainly marked on his face, he strode to the chair with as firm a tread as men ever walk on the last few steps of their lives.

The young man prayed softly during the process of strapping him in and affixing the electrodes. As the mask slipped over his face, I heard him murmur, "I'm innocent." With everything ready, I went to the instrument board, the officers backed away from the chair, and I threw the switch.

At the precise instant that the condemned man's body stiffened under the shock of 2,000 volts, something occurred that filled me with horror. The death-chamber telephone rang! I say it rang–I might rather say that it screamed. The telephone was only about a dozen feet from the electric chair, and a scant three or four feet from where I stood. It was as though the bell were right next to my ear, so loud did it sound to me in that otherwise quiet room.

I was transfixed, frozen. My heart seemed to stop beating. Through my mind flashed the story I had watched unfold on the screen just three days before, and my conversation with Mrs. Elliott. I remembered how I had expressed the hope that such an experience would never be mine. Had it now happened? Was I executing an innocent man?

My first instinctive thought when I heard the telephone was to turn off the current. But I knew that would do no good. Electricity had already shattered the man's nervous system, and was ripping through his straining body. Though all life was not yet gone, nothing could save him. If this were a last-second call from one in authority designed to snatch from the brink-of eternity the man whom the state had doomed, it had come too late. Perhaps a grim Fate had thrown at me an exact re-enactment of the motion picture I had seen. Yet, even should such have been the case, there was only one humane thing to do now: complete the execution.

As the telephone rang again, I glanced around the room. Everyone there was staring at me, wondering what I would do. My only action was to regulate the current.

Finally, the deputy warden, who had been standing near me, stepped to the telephone. He took the receiver from its hook, thus silencing the bell. The execution proceeded without further interruption.

At the end of a little more than two minutes-the longest and worst minutes I have ever experienced–I cut off the power. Limp and trembling, I prayed that there had been no mistake, that I had not this time executed a person who was innocent and was to have been spared. I hardly heard the physician's pronouncement that the man was dead.

The deputy warden walked over to the telephone, signaled the operator at the prison switchboard, and asked hoarsely, "What was that call?"

There was a reply, and the deputy warden hung up. Turning to me, he said: "It was nothing, Bob. The operator rang the wrong extension."

I felt greatly relieved. However, I hope that such a thing will never happen to me again.

In spite of every human effort to keep executions free of mishaps that throw even more than the necessary pall of horror over the room, accidents have occurred. For me, these death-chamber misadventures have provided unforgettable moments.

One of them took place at Sing Sing on a night that three Harlem men went to the chair. The men—Winston Owens, Joseph Willis, and Herman Cunningham—had killed a bartender in an attempted stick-up of a New York City cafe, and were put to death in the order named.

The first two executions were carried out without a hitch. Owens and Willis displayed no emotion as they sat down in the chair. The current, which for the first time came from the new power plant, regulated well, and the executions were as swift as any I have performed.

Then it was Cunningham's turn. He, also, was calm during his last seconds of life. After the customary final inspection of the chair, I moved to the controls. With the voltmeter registering 2,000 volts and everything apparently set, I threw the switch. But nothing happened. There was no lunging of the body against the straps, no crackle of current, no hiss or sparking of electrodes.

For a moment, I could not imagine what was wrong. I had tested the apparatus only a short time before, and found it working properly. Something else, therefore, was preventing the circuit from becoming complete. Opening the switch, I hastened to the chair.

A quick examination revealed the trouble. Because it evidently had not been screwed in securely, the wire had dropped out of the binding post of the leg electrode in the time I had walked from the chair to the switch. The act of replacing it was only a matter of seconds.

While I was doing this, I looked up at the condemned man to see if he had realized that there had been a delay.

He gave no indication that he had. He simply sat tense, awaiting the blow that was to hurl him into eternity. I returned to the instrument board, and closed the switch once more. This time the current shot through the prisoner.

There was almost a repetition of this unfortunate slip several years later. Again the place was Sing Sing, and again three men balanced the scales of justice with their lives. The near mishap occurred with the first prisoner to go. Just before turning on the current, I glanced back at the chair. My eye caught something amiss. The wire leading to the head electrode had slipped out. I remedied the situation immediately.

In Pennsylvania, as I have explained before, the electric chair must be tested in front of the witnesses. At the first execution which Rockview Penitentiary held at 12:30 A.M., I placed the Dank of twenty bulbs on the chair as usual after those who were to view the legal slaying had taken their places. When I switched on the current, the lights did not burn. I put the electrodes in a pail of water, and the current passed through it, proving that the apparatus was not faulty. Later, I discovered that a broken wire in the light circuit was responsible for the failure of the bulbs to illuminate.

Only once have I had to shut off the power before an electrocution was completed. For no reason that I can assign, the strap which was supposed to hold the leg electrode against the surface of the condemned man's skin had not been drawn tightly enough. When I reduced the current at the end of five seconds, I was horrified to see the electrode slip to the ankle. There, providing a poor contact, it sparked badly.

What I should do was perfectly clear. I opened the switch, and walked swiftly 'to the chair. In what may have seemed a long time to the witnesses, but in reality was only fifteen seconds, I had the electrode readjusted. The man's body, sagging with the abrupt cutoff of current, was insensible, but not yet lifeless. With the electrode now fitting snugly, I returned to the switch and closed it, thus bringing the ill-starred murderer's life ill-starred even in its final moments–to an end. The incident caused no consternation or commotion in the room.

At another time, just as the principal keeper was about to cover the condemned man's face with the mask, the helmet strap broke. It had seemed all right when examined it half an hour before, but apparently it was worn out. To wait until a new strap could be obtained would have meant delay and more mental anguish for the person in the chair. The principal keeper looked at me. I nodded for him to complete his task. Fortunately, the mask held the head electrode in place during the execution, but I had a most uneasy two and a quarter minutes. I do not believe that the prisoner or any of the witnesses knew what had happened.

Probably the most tense and difficult night for me was that of June 25, 1931. On that occasion, I was to execute two men, Haywood Turner and Frederick Innes, at Sing Sing for robbing and killing a man. Arriving at the prison shortly after six P.M., I was informed that the motor generator which supplied the current for electrocutions had burned out. Repaired, it failed a second time when tested. The Fates seemed doggedly determined to save two lives that had been demanded by the law.

With the hour for the executions fast approaching, prompt action was necessary. Someone suggested stringing wires into the prison from the outside power system, even though the current was at a higher voltage than is ordinarily sent to the chair there would not be sufficient time to put together a water rheostat with which to regulate the current, we would be obliged to use the electricity at its full strength. I warned the warden that this would result in considerable sparking and burning. But it was the only solution to the pressing problem before us, so the warden had the wires brought in.

All during the two executions, I was under a severe strain. There was little that I could do to eliminate burning of the bodies and the exceptional sparking that presented a particularly grisly death-room picture. In each case, however, I did turn off the current a few seconds before the customary time. Incidentally, this double execution was witnessed by a State Supreme Court justice, the first judge to attend an electrocution at which I officiated.

Three unusual things occurred at an execution in the New Jersey State Prison on the night of October 15, 1935-the first two when the condemned man traveled his "last mile"; the third after he was dead. The doomed prisoner was John Favorito, and he had murdered a gasoline station attendant in a holdup. The robbery had netted him and a companion only four dollars.

On his way to the electric chair at eight o'clock, Favorito passed the cell occupied by Bruno Richard Hauptmann, who was awaiting execution. If he had expected the Lindbergh kidnaper to call a farewell or some word of encouragement, he was disappointed. Hauptmann was sound asleep and snoring.

Favorito was bewildered as he entered the death chamber. Without a word, he proceeded slowly to the chair. While watching his movements, I noticed something very odd. He was walking in his bare feet.

After the current had coursed through the body for two and a quarter minutes, I turned it off. The prison physician applied a stethoscope over the man's heart, then jumped back, a startled expression on his face. He had received an electric shock. I stepped to the side of the chair, and touched the dead man's arm. I, too, got a shock. I glanced at the switch to see whether it was out. It was. Exactly what caused this is still a mystery, but I believe that moisture on the leads from the switch was responsible. Whatever it was, I have never had such an experience again.

Despite an occasional slip, electrocution, in my opinion, is the most humane method of capital punishment that has been devised. Besides being swift, sure, and painless, as well as less gruesome for the witnesses, it has another great advantage—the condemned person is not cognizant of a mishap, even should one occur. If the failure is one of wires, the current simply does not reach

183

him, and he is unaware of the mistake. If the initial shock strikes him, he is rendered unconscious, and would know or feel nothing that might happen.

This is not true of hanging. There have been numerous cases in which an accident, due to miscalculation or bungling, has caused the condemned person untold physical and mental suffering. For instance, few people have met a more dreadful death at the hands of the law than the Apache Indian who was hanged by the Federal Government at San Carlos, Arizona, in 1936.

The improvised gallows was an old rock crusher, which had been employed in the construction of Coolidge Dam. A rope was tied to a cross beam, and a hole was cut in the floor for a trap. When the victim was dropped, his body struck the side of the trap, and the knot of the noose slipped. His neck was not broken. For a long time, the man kicked and groaned as life was agonizingly squeezed out of him by strangulation. It was more than half an hour before he was pronounced dead.

Less serious, but still torturous for two doomed men, was the premature springing of the trap at a triple execution at the West Virginia State Penitentiary in 1938. Two of the trio were hanged simultaneously. Before the noose could be placed on one, the platform on which he was standing opened, and he fell twelve feet to the concrete floor. Though partly stunned, he managed to smile when guards picked him up and carried him back. Then he had to go through the ordeal of watching his executioners test and retest the trap catch. All during this time, his companion stood silently by with the noose around his neck.

Many times the rope has come off or broken when a poor wretch shot through the trap, necessitating dropping him again. On a number of other occasions, the head has been jerked from the body. An executioner in Canada lost his job after this happened to a woman whom he hanged.

Some experts claim that death by gas is the most merciful way of legally killing criminals. Yet witnesses to such executions dispute this contention. They have described the horrible facial expression and contortions of the condemned, how his consciousness fought the deadly fumes for several minutes, how his heart beat even after life appeared to have departed. A newspaperman told me that, peering through the thick glass window of the lethal chamber, he carried on a lip-reading conversation with a victim four and a half minutes after the cyanide pellets were dropped in the acid.

The State of North Carolina once had occasion to use the gas chamber and the electric chair on the same day. Two desperadoes were put to death by asphyxiation, adopted by the state in 1935. Another murderer was electrocuted because his crime had been committed and sentence passed before the new law. Following the executions, newspapermen who had viewed them were questioned by the governor as to which form they considered the more humane. The majority favored the electric chair.

That the bloody guillotine brings fast and certain death is undeniable. But the act of dismembering the head from the body is a barbarous thing that has no place in a supposedly enlightened civilization. A man is entitled to something approaching dignity as he leaves this world, and dignity is certainly far removed from the act of decapitation.

Execution by a firing squad, as is sometimes the means in Utah, has one objectionable feature. The bullets may fail to hit a vital spot, with the result that death is not instantaneous and the condemned may suffer pain before he succumbs.

No, if we must have capital punishment, I am convinced that the method of which I am a practitioner is by all odds the most humane and most seemly. I feel confident that nearly every condemned person, if permitted a choice, would elect death by electricity in preference to any other.

LETTERS TO AN EXECUTIONER

My mail has been described as "the world's strangest." Perhaps it is. Certainly it is entirely unlike that received by most people.

By far the greater number of the letters I get are from individuals unknown to me. They come from men and women in all walks of life and in all parts of the world. Even children write me. I read all the letters, but answer few of them. The reason for this will be seen when I quote some typical ones.

Whenever an execution attracts public attention and brings my name into the news, there is a great increase in my mail. The letters are addressed either to my home or to the prisons in the states I serve. Believing that its contents might cause my family and me uneasiness and worry, the prison authorities occasionally keep a letter from me. However, this is not done very frequently.

As I have said before, threats of violence are not uncommon. They do not particularly alarm me, for I am convinced that the great majority are products of erratic but comparatively harmless minds. Sometimes these notes are general in character, but more often refer to specific cases. They bear nothing to identify the writers; consequently, I have no way of knowing whether they are from relatives or friends of the condemned persons, or

186

merely sympathizers. Take this unsigned one, for example:

Your daughter will die just like you killed Irene Schroeder.

Here is another which came from Newark, New Jersey, a week or so before a quadruple execution at the state prison in Trenton:

Don't pull the switch to kill the four men who are innocent. If you do, your days are numbered.

There was a follow-up several days later:

This is our last warning. Take heed or you die.

Ornamented with a skull and crossbones, a message scrawled in red ink informed me:

You gave Joe his medicine, now you will get yours. Hide all you want, but it won't do you any good. You are done for.

This one, from "The Black Hand Gang," was dated January 13, 1928–the day after Ruth Snyder and Judd Gray went to the chair:

Dog Elliott: You dirty, filthy ----, you should drop dead long ago, for you are a cold-blooded butcher and murderer. Also Warden Lawes better look out and watch his step. You better resign your job at once if you care to live much longer. Also your friend, the warden. Also the state doctor ought to be in hell long ago. The black hand will get you all sooner or later. Beware all of you.

Such a letter is no cause for real concern because it is obviously an empty threat. It is possible, of course, that the man or men who sent that letter planted the bomb which blew up my house four months later. But I hardly think so. The human snake is not likely to rattle a warning before he strikes.

I seem to be a good target for invectiveness of the worst kind, and have been labeled about everything obnoxious and loathsome. Murderer, fiend, butcher–these are the terms most commonly employed to describe me. When my critics have run out of words, they have coined a few of their own. Women especially derive some peculiar pleasure from heaping abuse upon my head. From Philadelphia, one wrote:

You won't like what I am going to say to you, but I am going to tell you how I feel just the same. You are a disgrace to your family and to all mankind. It is bad enough that you kill, but you murder for money, and that makes your crime that much more terrible.

I don't believe you have a heart. If you have, it must be made of stone. You must be very cruel or you couldn't take human life like you do. You will be punished for the horrible things you have done, and I hope you will suffer as much as you have made other people suffer.

Calling me a "barbarian and cannibal," a young lady in Allentown, Pennsylvania, added:

I think you are the worst specimen of a man. Everybody should shun you like they would some awful creature. You are not fit to live with human beings, and I can't imagine any who would want to associate with you. I for one would cross the street if I saw you coming toward me.

A New York man expressed his opinion of me in the following language:

I cannot restrain myself from writing to you of the ways and means you have acquired in the manner which makes you a living. From what I understand, you are at a time of life when men have more knowledge of the ways of the world, and to think that there is an individual who really would turn on a current that would send humans to their death in such a brutal manner.

You ought to bury your face in the dirt. If there is any manly principle left in your inhuman carcass, you should blowout your brains, if you have any. I would not do your rotten work for any price. I could not be hired for such a purpose for all they could give me in this world. I would be ashamed to let the sun shine on me or to breathe the fresh air. You are worse than the criminals you send to their doom.

How can you look a man in the face? How can you raise children? How can you look your wife or relatives in the face and call yourself a man? If you cannot get a living any other way, you ought to starve to death, you poor, miserable cur. What kind of a thinking mind have you, anyhow?

188

Shortly after I put the Lindbergh kidnaper to death, a Columbia University student dropped me this note:

A friend of mine asked me yesterday what I thought about Hauptmann's execution. I told him. I also told him what I thought of you, but I do not believe you would care to hear that. It was not very flattering, you can be sure.

But a man in Buffalo, New York, was not so considerate of my feelings when he said:

I read in the papers where you executed over three hundred people. You are the same as your victims - a murderer. It does not make any difference that you did it as a job for the state. When you die, nobody will shed a tear. There will be only cursing after you. It is a wonder to me that somebody hasn't sent a bullet into you.

Although I am sorry that many people harbor such ill will toward me, I am not troubled by letters of this sort. At first, they did disturb me; but now I have come to expect and accept them.

I often ponder the protests which are sent me in the name of religion. The authors are usually clergymen, church workers, or other earnest men and women. Witness this one from a distressed New England minister:

For more than thirty years, I have preached the Gospel wherever I have gone. I have taught obedience to the Ten Commandments. "Thou shalt not kill" is one of these. By your deeds, you have broken this many, many times.

Some day we will all have to appear before Almighty God and account for our sins upon the earth. I beg of you to stop the terrible thing you are doing. Spend your remaining years in prayer for the Lord's forgiveness. He is merciful and kind, and He will hear your prayers. Do it now before it is too late. This is my plea to you.

One woman asked, "How can you press the button of electricity to send people to their death?" She continued:

It is murder. You or anyone else who does that in the sight of God is doing wrong. Think upon this, you do it for money. God's eyes go up and down over the earth. Think of your taking hundreds of lives.

189

Another communication along the same line from an elderly woman in Meridian, Mississippi, is quoted in part:

You seem to think that you can kill those poor unfortunates because the law, made by man and not God, says that you can, and get by with no blame attached to yourself. But according to God's divine law, you are guilty along with the others. "Thou shalt not kill" applies to the innocent person as well as to the criminal. God's law denies man the right to kill man, no matter what the circumstances might be. Whether you believe it or not, you cannot kill those poor creatures, no matter how guilty they are, and not be responsible to your Creator..

How would you feel if one of those men whom your hand sends into eternity were your boy? Well, they are some fathers' boys. You may not believe it, but right now you stand guilty before the Creator of us all of those poor creatures' deaths. You may escape earthly laws and the vengeance of those who are bitter toward you, but you won't escape the just punishment meted out to all of us who trample God's laws under our feet. No excuse that we may offer will save us.

Some day, sometime, both you and your family will suffer the same as others who break God's laws and try to hide behind excuses. God is going to require their blood at your hands.

I believe that I should rather receive letters of this type than the one from a man in Tulsa, Oklahoma. He wrote me on the day following Hauptmann's execution:

Good for you, Mr. Elliott. Don't ever let your conscience bother you about spinning the wheel of the rheostat that sent 2,000 volts of electricity through the body of Bruno Richard Hauptmann. Hauptmann got exactly what was coming to him when he was electrocuted.

That note indicated pleasure in death. It also showed vengeance. It explained better than any words of mine why capital punishment endures, why it may continue for many years.

I have never been able to understand why .anyone should want my autograph. Yet I am besieged by requests for my signature, especially just before and immediately after I have executed a well-known person. Here is a sample letter:

190

I know you are the official executioner for New Jersey who will send the fatal current through Bruno Richard Hauptmann when he goes to the electric chair this week. I am writing to ask you for your autograph. I have autographs of many prominent men, such as J. Edgar Hoover, Warden Lewis E. Lawes and others, including another executioner. I hope you will send me your autograph. I wish you good luck.

A few days later, a mother in Washington, New Jersey, asked:

Will you kindly honor my little girl and I by autographing the two enclosed cards? We would like to have your autograph in our books, but on account of the cost of mailing, we are sending cards instead of the books. We would like your own handwriting.

Please, Mr. Elliott, don't disappoint us, as we have Governor Hoffman's and all of the lawyers on both sides of the Hauptmann case, and we would like to have yours also.

Applications for the post of executioner or that of my assistant constitute a surprisingly large part of my mail. There are several reasons why the writers seek such an appointment. One is apparently a strange desire to kill, and another is the notoriety attending this unusual occupation. The most predominant is the need of money. A few of these people, of course, are deeply interested in electricity and its various uses; but they are very much in the minority.

After stating that he wished to impress me with his sincerity, a middle-aged man in Fairland, Indiana, went on:

It has been a lifelong ambition of mine to be an executioner. I have no fanatical desire or publicity stunt in mind in wishing to enter this line of work. It has been a hobby of mine for years, experimenting with electricity in destroying animals, and I have worked for the most humane executions by electricity.

He then described himself as having "a good appearance and personality," and outlined what he believed were his qualifications. These included a college degree in science and membership in the Christian Church. He applied for employment as my assistant.

Another man, in Los Angeles, California, wrote:

According to the newspaper reports, I understand you are the official executioner of Sing Sing Prison. While I know the life of an executioner is perhaps not a pleasant one, someone has to carry out the law.

Have you an assistant or anyone who can replace you when you do not feel able to go on with your work?

I am thirty-six years old, and am a single man with no one to care what happens to me or where I go. As to my education, I would say that it is fair.

If you could use me as an assistant, I will be glad to hear from you at your convenience.

A resident of Salem, Massachusetts, who had communicated with me before, sent a second plea:

I really meant what I said in my letter about wanting the job as executioner. The reason I am asking you to get the job for me is that I don't know who to go to ask for it. It wouldn't take me long to learn how to do the work. All I would have to do is see you do it once. If you could arrange to have me with you on one of these jobs, it would give me an idea of what I would have to do.

I am having a hard time trying to make a living for my wife and son. I'm not making enough to pay my bills arid buy food. That is why I am asking you to help me this way.

Even more pitiful was a letter dated March 6, 1936, from Springfield, Massachusetts:

I am writing you a few lines which I sincerely hope and pray you will read and give your earliest consideration.

First, I want to say that the job of executioner must be filled by a man of middle age, as it is no job for a young, flighty man. The man must have one hundred per cent perfect nerves; he must be a man of great integrity; he must be alert and prompt on his calls; he must have no sympathy for the man or woman who is about to meet his or her fate; he must be a man who can keep his place and keep his mouth closed as to what goes on, and perform his duty only for the sake of justice and the safety of humanity; he must be a man of good character, and he must be a man who does his duty for justice and society and not for a thrill. . . .

I am a man fifty-one years old. I haven't worked for three years, and it is impossible for a man of my age to get work in Massachusetts. I draw a small pension of $34 a month as an ex-soldier. I was not in the war, but was shot at target practice. I used to get $60, but they took half of it away under President Roosevelt's economy act, and they expect me to live on that with a family of six with myself. I cannot get aid because I draw this $34 pension.

I don't want my children to grow up and support me. I want to support them and give them an education. We are good Christian people, belong to the Baptist Church and believe in what is right and in Jesus Christ our Savior. I don't see why a man should be turned down from work because he is fifty-one years old and able to support his family.

Now, Mr. Elliott, if you are ever in Springfield, I wish you would come to see me and have a talk. This is what I wish you would try to do for me: if you ever make up your mind to retire, which I read in the papers you intend to do soon, will you please help me to secure your position. I am sure you will never regret it, and you would be helping a man who is craving to make his family happy by supporting them properly. My wife is crippled and cannot help me, and my children are undernourished for the want of more substantial food.

Oh, Mr. Elliott, won't you please help me to get your position if you resign. I would be so thankful to you, and would be able to smile once more with the thought that I would be earning a living for my little family. If you do this, I know God will thank you as I would from the bottom of my heart. Hoping you will consider this letter at your earliest convenience, I will close by wishing you good health and a long life of happiness.

In September, 1927, a man in Trenton, New Jersey, who had put several prisoners to death for a Western state volunteered his services in the event that I should be unable to report for a scheduled execution. His proposal was this:

Perhaps there will be times when you would desire a man to substitute for you due to sickness or other causes. I have carried out electrocutions myself, and have been an applicant for the work in all four states that you operate for since the early part of 1922, but, for some reason or another, I didn't get any. I am an expert and understand the business thoroughly, and any time you wish to substitute me in your place, I would be willing to do so..

Say, for instance, if old age overtakes you or you should desire to retire from the business, you would confer a favor on me by giving me an opportunity to take up where you leave off. It's a thing that has to be done, and I consider that I may as well do it as anyone else whenever or wherever I can get the work.

I'm strictly temperate, forty-three years of age and a native of this state. I trust that I will hear from you, Mr. Elliott, in reply to this letter. I am the same as yourself and no trifler. It is strictly a business matter with me. Please let me hear from you in the future.

When this man received no encouragement from me, he communicated with Governor A. Harry Moore of New Jersey. "I will accept this work for $300 a year, disregarding the number of electrocutions, or I will fill the job and carry out the electrocutions for $100 a head," he wrote the governor. His offer was promptly rejected.

Incidentally, a former public official in Massachusetts gave that state an opportunity to reduce its cost of executing murderers. He told a legislative committee that he would be glad to throw the switch any time for five dollars. "I'd like a job like that," he said.

One day in 1936, I received a request from a young girl in Waseca, Minnesota, for technical facts about electrocutions. She was so sincere that I furnished her with the information. Nearly two years later, she communicated with me again. After thanking me for "having bothered to answer what, according to mother, was a silly letter," the girl asked a most amazing question:

I'm graduating from high school, and I haven't yet made up my mind concerning what I want to do. Would you recommend getting a job like yours?

Many people would have me use my influence to obtain invitations for them to witness executions. I consistently refuse to do this, and usually advise them to apply to the warden of the prison where they wish to see the death penalty exacted. If they follow my suggestion

194

and fail to get a reply, I frequently hear from them again. That is what happened in this case:

When do you think we will be able to get our invitation to an execution at Sing Sing? We put in an application, me and my friend, the time I received your letter, and we did as you said, but we have not heard anything yet.

Please, Mr. Elliott, see if you could help us in some way so we could see one in the near future. We would appreciate it very much if you would be so kind as to help us out.

Information which they believe I can supply is sought by some who write me. For instance, a clergyman in Milton, Oregon, desired the names of the chaplains who attended Ruth Snyder and Judd Gray on their "last mile." It seemed that a minister who was not present at the double execution was claiming in a lecture that he had been the chaplain on that occasion. The clergyman who communicated with me was anxious to learn the truth.

In the same mail came a letter from a man in Nashville, Tennessee, who had been told that I had executed a friend of his. The friend had left for the East two years previously, he said, and had not been heard from since. There was a rumor that he had committed a serious crime in Pennsylvania. I was glad to inform this man that I knew nothing of his friend.

Advocates and opponents of capital punishment set forth their views in letters to me. A Tracy City, Tennessee, lawyer, who had both prosecuted and defended murderers, upheld the extreme penalty in the following manner:

Our legislators passed the statute providing the death penalty as punishment for certain defined crimes. I am of the opinion that the punishment as established was enacted for the purpose of restraining a potential murderer on the theory that his contemplation of the punishment decreed might act as a deterrent in his contemplation of the commission of such a crime. Whether or not this is the case, the fact remains that for the crime the punishment is provided. And the punishment having been provided, lack of its enforcement would leave us with no threatened penalty for the crime whatever.

I'll admit that the death of the murderer can in no way restore to life the murdered one. But the penalty was provided before the murder was committed, and if it is to serve its purpose as a restraining agent, the penalty must be enforced. I am of the opinion that the more severe and inescapable the penalty, the less will society be annoyed by the crime, and as such I am actually in favor of severe penalties as an object lesson to future murderers. I am in favor of the death penalty being administered publicly to increase the force of the object lesson. Harsh? Certainly, but so is murder.

As a rule, women who write me do not approve the taking of life by law. However, a mother in Seattle, Washington, feels differently. She argued:

We kill rabid animals, and some humans are as dangerous as rabid animals. I am a firm believer in capital punishment. We are taxed to care for criminals who would be better off out of this world. I do believe that the lethal chamber is the most humane, but again there are some criminals who do not fear death that is easy. They fear the "hot squat," as criminals call the electric chair.

I am a mother, and have a son I love devotedly; but should he break a law that called for his death, I should not blame his executioner. I believe that the raising of children has a very great deal to do in what they turn out to be. I have taught my son truth, honor and honesty, and taught him that he has to pay for his errors.

Perhaps the reason that so many people are unwilling to serve on juries in capital cases is explained in a note from a resident of Union City, Pennsylvania. It read:

For many years now, I have not believed in capital punishment. I could not be one of those to judge any man in such a case, as I would look upon myself as a more coldblooded murderer in heart than the unfortunate one who may have committed the deed in a fit of anger, or revenge, et cetera.

That the electric chair is the most merciful instrument of death is the conviction of a great many who send letters to me. A number have reached this conclusion after watching condemned prisoners executed by different methods. Said a man in Raleigh, North Carolina:

As a newspaperman, it has been my unpleasant experience to witness a number of electrocutions, several asphyxiations, and one hanging, and I am firm in my belief that the electric chair is far more humane than the gas chamber.

An ex-reporter, of Milton, Pennsylvania, wrote

My first job was with a newspaper. Hanging was then the means of inflicting the death penalty in Pennsylvania. Electrocution had not yet been adopted. There was to be an execution at our county prison, and my boss asked me if I would represent the paper and write the article. I accepted. I witnessed the execution and fulfilled my duty. I decided then and there that hanging is certainly no humane way of inflicting capital punishment.

Mr. Elliott, I sincerely agree with you that if we are to have capital punishment, it should be inflicted quickly and humanely. Electrocution is absolutely the only method.

Yet, in the eyes of a few, the chair is too quick, too humane. These people believe that murderers should be made to suffer slow torture for their crimes. This is the horrible punishment one person suggested:

Have his legs tied together, his hands bound behind him, and a rope under his armpits to support his weight above a boiling tank of sulphuric acid. The end of the rope should be fastened to a device which would lower the victim into this tank slowly. The tank should be floodlighted so the victim could see the penalty he had to pay for his crime.

Sympathetic understanding is expressed in some of the letters I get. For instance, my photograph in a magazine prompted the following from a resident of Corinth, Mississippi:

I am struck with the lines of care and suffering depicted on your face. Now I know what suffering means, and I want to express my deep sympathy with anyone who suffers in any way.

Let me say that I do not look upon you as any different from the rest of society. The people make the laws, and as regards capital punishment, they are really carrying out the decrees of God Himself. Someone has to do the distasteful work of putting criminals out of the way. We citizens ought to back up our public servants in every way. You are just as much one of us as if you had never been chosen to do your gravely important work.

Please continue to be cheerful, and remember that the majority of right-thinking citizens are backing you up.

Now and then I receive a letter from an ex-convict whom I have befriended or who was assigned to the powerhouse at Clinton Prison while I was chief engineer there. Here is one from a former inmate who now lives in Yonkers, New York:

Friend Bob: I have been trying to find your address for a long time, but didn't get it until now. I am home now going on six years, married and have two kids. Believe me, I am very happy. I am working at steam fitting–that is, when I can get work, for this sure was a tough year. Bob, how are your children and the Missus?

Man, I feel bully. This sure is better than working in the powerhouse for a cent and a half a day. I sure would like to see you and the family. Many a handout I ate in your house in Clinton. But no more prison for me.

From another ex-convict who followed the much-quoted advice to young men about going West came this:

It has been a long time since I last wrote you, but don't think for a single minute that I have forgotten your many kindnesses to me. When I got out of Clinton, I worked in New York for three years and then headed West. I've been out here ever since, and am doing well by myself. I have a wife and family, and nobody knows out here about my being in prison. Everybody treats me fine, and I try to treat them the same way.

I hope you and yours are enjoying the best of everything. You deserve all the happiness you can get, because you've always helped others when they needed it most. You sure did help me, and I'll always thank you for it. If you're ever out in this part of the world, be sure and look me up. I'd certainly like to see you again.

While I was seriously ill one time, the fact was mentioned over the air by a radio commentator. As a result, I received several hundred cards and letters, all hoping that I would soon be well again. A minister in Spotswood, New Jersey, sent "prayers and best wishes for a speedy recovery," and a Newark,

New Jersey, woman said that "lots of folks 'are thinking of and hoping only best for you." Another well-wisher would have me "spared for many years to continue your obedient service to the state."

Along with these kind expressions was this note from Washington, D. C.:

I do not know you or your family, I am sorry to say, but I wrote you a few years ago when you were so cruelly written up in the newspapers. I am glad you did not give up your job. It is one of the most important in the country. I was glad to read in today's paper that you are much improved in health, and I feel sure you have many happy years ahead for yourself and Mrs. Elliott.

MY PRIVATE LIFE

Friendless, lonely, a social outcast. That, according to common supposition, is the miserable existence that is mine. I know this from letters I receive and from stories published about me. I know it, too, from my own contacts with others.

It has been said that, shunned by neighbors and relatives, I am a recluse, living in an atmosphere of funereal gloom and venturing out only when it is absolutely necessary. When I do appear in public, rumor has it, people run from me as they would the plague. In short, I am a man who literally "walks alone."

This popular impression of how I live has no foundation in truth. Except when interrupted by the state's order that I put another human being to death, my life is a prosaic and pleasant one. It differs little from that of the average man.

I am, of course, fully aware of the fact that people generally look down on the occupation of official executioner. I am reminded of a statement attributed to the late Henri Anatole Deibler, for many years France's headsman:

"To kill in the name of one's country is a glorious feat, one rewarded by medals. But to kill in the name of the law, that is a gruesome, horrible function, rewarded with scorn, contempt, and loathing."

200

Society insists on the death penalty for certain serious crimes, and expects the sentence of the court to be carried out. Someone must act as the last human agency of the law. Yet, the man designated for this great responsibility is regarded in the manner so aptly described by M. Deibler.

Not long ago, a friend came to visit me. When he got off the train at the station, he took a taxi, giving the driver the address of my home. On reaching the house, the driver remarked: "Say, buddy, this can't be the place. You don't want to go there."

"And why not?" inquired my friend.

"Why that's where Elliott, the executioner, lives." My friend assured the driver that this was his destination. As the surprised man drove off, he was heard to mumble to himself, "I hope he knows what he's doing."

Shortly after I was appointed as Pennsylvania's executioner, I obtained some firsthand information as to the sentiment against me. Returning on the train from Bellefonte one day, I sat next to an elderly man. We struck up a conversation, during which he said, "I saw the fellow on the station platform at Tyrone who executed a man at the prison this morning."

"You don't say," I replied. "What kind of a chap was he?"

"Oh, he looked like he wouldn't mind killing people," the passenger answered. "It was written all over his face. No wonder nobody bothers with him."

"Somebody once told me that he isn't as bad as he's pictured," I said, "that he's just the same as you and I."

"Humph, that's a good one," grunted the man. "Nobody can make me believe that. Anybody who can do his job isn't human. Nope, he's not like us."

At that, we dropped the subject. He had not recognized me, and I did not introduce myself.

This man and the cab driver plainly indicated the public attitude toward me. Undesirable as it is, I have not permitted it to interfere with my happiness and that of my family. We live as other people do, enjoying most of the comforts and pleasures of life.

I have been very fortunate in my home life. My wife has always been devoted and understanding. No father has received more attention and consideration from his children. I am sure I have their affection and respect. Never once have they attempted to conceal from others the fact that I am their father. I do not believe that such a thing has ever entered their minds.

At the prisons I serve, most of the officials and attendants are cordial to me. Several occasionally visit my home, and I carryon a correspondence with a few of them. But there was a chaplain who avoided me as much as possible. This was because he was so bitterly opposed to capital punishment and the important role I play in it. When we did meet, he would pass by without the slightest sign of recognition. His behavior, however, did not change my high regard for him and his splendid work among the prisoners.

As for neighbors, I could not ask for better ones. They are sociable, thoughtful, and co-operative. When our home was bombed, they came to our aid without a moment's hesitation. If there is illness in the family, they inquire as to how things are, and whether they can be of any help. Some drop in now and then for an evening of bridge or just to talk. Of course, we, too, have always tried to be good neighbors.

I believe I have a number of friends–real friends. Among them are men of prominence. One of my good friends is the pastor of the church of which Mrs. Elliott and I are members. He frequently calls on us, and sometimes comes for dinner, on which occasions my wife prepares his favorite dish–Boston baked beans.

My son and two daughters, all happily married, have as many friends as any young people should have. So far as I know, they have never suffered because I am an executioner. At no time have they voiced an objection to my unusual occupation or asked me to give it up. If I had thought I could not manage the work without handicapping them and their outlook on life, I should not have considered it. Moreover, I would have resigned just as soon as I saw that happening.

As it is, I cannot see that what I do has made their lives any different from what they would have been if I had become the Methodist minister my parents wanted me to be.

Only once has my work for the state caused the feelings of any member of the family to be hurt. It happened to Clarabelle, my little granddaughter who is nicknamed "Pat." She was playing with a group of children when one of the girls said to her, "Your granddaddy is a bad man."

Pat vehemently denied the charge.

"But he is," insisted her playmate. "He kills people. My daddy read it in the paper."

Tears crept into Pat's usually laughing brown eyes. She ran home as fast as her legs could carry her, and straightway sought out her mother, who is my daughter, Frances.

"Mommy," she asked, "is my Bompa a bad man?" My wife has always been "Born" and I have been "Bompa" to our several grandchildren.

"No, indeed, Pat," replied her mother. "But why do you ask such a question?"

Pat sobbed out her story. "I told the girls Bompa was a nice man, but they said he wasn't," she added.

My daughter sat down with Pat, then nine years old, and explained deliberately and carefully one of the tragic facts of our complex civilization. She pointed out that there are people in this world against whom the others must be protected. She told her that some commit terrible crimes in spite of the law, and must be punished. I am the man, she continued, who has been appointed to carry out the order of the court in six states after it has been decided that a person must pay for his crime with his life.

"It's much better that somebody like Bompa do this work than some other sort of man," Pat's mother said. "You know he is kind and loves children. He doesn't like to kill people. He is simply doing what the law says has to be done."

I believe Pat understood her mother's explanation. She has been to see me many times since then, but has never mentioned the incident. So far as I can tell, her affection for me has remained unchanged.

A story which is forever bobbing up is to the effect that merchants will not accept my money. The reason given is that they consider it "blood money." To hurdle this obstacle, so the story runs, I must get other people to do my buying. This is just another of the ridiculous tales that are circulated about me. No person has ever refused my money, or taken the trouble to inquire as to its source. We have had the same grocer for more than twenty years, the vegetable man for ten years, the butcher for eight years, and so on down the line of tradesmen.

One duty of a citizen that I have not performed is serving on a jury. But I was called for such service a few years ago in Queens County, New York. I reported at the office of the clerk, presented the notice, and revealed that I held the position of state executioner. I was promptly excused, and assured that I would never be troubled again.

Frankly, I am glad of this. There is nothing I would hate more than to be charged with the duty of deciding whether a human being is to live or die. Sitting on a jury that brought in a verdict demanding the death penalty, I would feel incomparably more responsible for the taking of a life than I ever have felt as the person whose hand controls the switch which sends current to the electric chair.

When not acting as the state's agent of death or doing electrical contracting jobs, I spend a great deal of time in my flower garden. I am particularly proud of my roses and gladioli, which have been the envy of the neighborhood. Children often gather around me when I appear in the back yard, and sometimes accompany me on a short stroll.

I have a motion picture camera with which I "shoot" my grandchildren at play, and they like to be actors in these little skits. They can hardly curb their impatience until the films are developed and returned to me. Then we have a movie show of our own, and I frequently have to repeat a popular scene several times.

The outdoors has always held a great attraction for me—probably because I was brought up on a farm. Besides walking in the woods, I am especially fond of fishing. I do this off Long Island Sound with my son and two sons-in-law, and could relate many a "fish" story.

In the evening, my diversions are varied. Although we are not avid movie fans, my wife and I go to the theater occasionally. She enjoys romantic pictures and musicals; my choice is comedies. However, we have no difficulty in agreeing on a feature which will appeal to both of us.

At home, when no one has dropped in for a visit, I usually read or listen to the radio. I like to read, preferring non-fiction. Biographies of men famous in history interest me most. I do pick up a detective story, but these are not ordinarily on my list. Unlike John Hulbert, my predecessor, I do not purposely avoid crime news for fear I will learn something about a person I may be called upon to execute. On the other hand, stories of this nature do not highlight my newspaper reading.

For a laugh, I turn to the newspaper comics. I read them to my son and daughters when they were young-sters, and now I must do the same for my grandchildren when they come to the house. As a result, glancing over the funnies has become a habit. My favorite comics are "Mr. and Mrs." and "Regular Fellers." The fact that Jimmie Dugan (the principal character in the latter strip) has never grown a bit has always amused me.

Radio programs which test one's knowledge are the most popular with me. Especially true is this of the question-and-answer variety and spelling-bees. Sports, news, and music are my next three preferences in the order given.

Nearly everyone has an idol, some public figure whom he admires above all others—perhaps an important officeholder, a movie star, an athlete, or an author. Mine was Will Rogers. In my opinion, he was one of the most human, most natural individuals who ever lived. The world is better for men like him. His dry humor and homey philosophy struck a responsive chord in me, and I read what he wrote and heard his radio broadcasts at every opportunity. It was as though I had lost a friend when I learned of the airplane crash which took Will Rogers' life.

I was also a great admirer of President Coolidge. Once, while in Massachusetts, I drove by his home in Northampton, and was rewarded by seeing him on the porch. The only President I have met was Benjamin Harrison, who was still in office at the time. I was just a boy then, and never forgot how tightly he clasped my hand.

Excepting my family, my car has afforded me my greatest pleasure in recent years. I thoroughly enjoy driving, and even on my trips to the prisons, go by automobile whenever possible. Only twice have I had a misadventure in the car, and one of these barely escaped being serious.

On that particular day, in 1933, I was on my way to Rockview Penitentiary. Mrs. Elliott was with me. She often goes along to Bellefonte because she likes the Nittany Mountains, and usually remains in a hotel or a little inn we have discovered in a neighboring town until I return to pick her up. Then we drive back home by easy stages.

We left the house that morning about 5:45 o'clock in a new car which I had just bought. We had not driven more than ten minutes when the accident occurred. At a crossing, one of the rear wheels of our car was struck by a speeding automobile. Our machine turned over, imprisoning us inside. People near by righted our car, and helped us get out.

My wife and I were bruised and badly shaken, and my left shoulder was painfully wrenched. The car, considerably damaged, was pushed across the street to a garage, where the fender was straightened and the broken wheel replaced. There was not time enough to repair a huge dent in the top of the car.

The accident did not particularly upset me or Mrs. Elliott, We continued our trip, and at Bellefonte the prison physician gave us sedatives. I performed the execution the next morning, after which we drove to Western New York for a week's vacation.

On another occasion shortly afterward, I was en route to Sing Sing, something under a two-hour drive from my home. I was not late, but was half an hour or so behind my anticipated schedule. I admit I was wasting no time. At a street intersection, I crowded a traffic light which showed red, and was signaled to the curb by a stern-faced motorcycle policeman, who had come up behind me.

"What's your hurry?" he demanded. "What do you want to do–kill somebody?"

"Officer," I replied, "I'm sorry to say that's exactly what I'm going to do. In fact, I'll have to cause the death of two men tonight."

He stepped back with an exclamation as I hastened to reveal my identity and mission.

"All right," he said, "get along with you. But mind you watch those red lights. They're not just ornaments, you know."

In my travels, I rarely reveal my identity. This is not because I am ashamed of my occupation, or because I wish to be mysterious. I have other reasons. For one thing, I have no desire to seem to exploit my connection with legal death, which is such a fascinating subject to so many people. For another, strangers who depend on distorted writings and rumors for their impressions of me might be uneasy in my presence were they to know who I, am. I should not want this to happen.

There was one time in Pennsylvania when I yielded to an impulse: I disclosed my identity to a man and his wife. But even then I waited until the last minute before I told them. The incident occurred while I was on my way

207

home after putting a prisoner to death at Rockview Penitentiary.

Mrs. Elliott and I had decided to stay at a tourist house for the night. The proprietor and his wife were nice, chatty folks, who proved to be good hosts. As we were the only people stopping there, we sat around talking during the evening.

The conversation, not unnaturally, drifted to the execution performed that morning and featured in the afternoon newspaper which our host had been scanning. The executed man had been a native of that locality, and had formerly been a hard-working citizen. But he had killed, and I suppose he deserved the electric chair–if anyone does.

"He certainly had it coming to him," commented my host, and there was an almost vengeful tone in his voice. "He was a cold-blooded murderer. I don't know how that executioner felt about it, but I could gladly have thrown the switch on that fellow myself."

I never like to hear people say that sort of thing. He did not, of course, know that I was the man who actually had thrown the switch.

"I think I can understand how you feel," I said, "but your attitude is one of the things that are wrong with capital punishment. The tendency too often is toward vengeance, rather than justice and the control of crime."

We continued the discussion for a while, and this otherwise pleasant, generous man was almost hard in his insistence that "the only way to handle people like that is to kill them off. Then we're sure they'll not do it again."

I did not press the point further. He was a fisherman, and we forgot capital punishment in talking about the trout he had caught a day or two before in, a near-by stream.

The next morning, as Mrs. Elliott and I were about to leave, I said to our hosts:

"I have a little surprise for you. When we were discussing capital punishment and the execution last night, I thought it best not to tell you who I am. I was afraid that if I did, you might not be able to sleep. I'm the one who executed that man yesterday morning. That's why I expressed myself so freely on the subject."

I have rarely seen more surprised people, and I thought the woman drew back just a little. But her husband simply laughed.

"It wouldn't have bothered me a bit, Mr. Elliott," he said. "There's only one way to treat murderers, and somebody's got to do it. I hope you'll come to see us again on your next trip to the prison."

As I have tried to show, my years have been spent with life as well as with death. They have, for the most part, been happy ones. My work has not affected the course of my life or my outlook on life in general. It has not hardened me toward humanity or made me callous. If anything, I have come to realize the importance and value of so many little things which are likely to escape our attention.

DEATH IS NOT THE ANSWER

Am I a murderer?

A great many people are convinced that I am. They say that when I end a life with searing suddenness by throwing an electric switch, I am in the class with those whom I execute. I am, they insist, as truly a murderer as the gangster whose bullet finds its mark, as the man or woman who schemingly kills for money, as the depraved sex fiend who slays a little child. The fact that I am inflicting punishment for a horrible crime, that my act is authorized and directed by law, makes no difference to them.

I cannot subscribe to this contention, for I do not feel that I am a murderer. Had I believed for a single second that I was, I would have given up the grim work immediately. I carefully thought it all out before accepting the post of executioner–yes, even before I quite unexpectedly was called upon to put to death my first man on that early morning in 1904.

Each time I send a human being hurtling into eternity to face final judgment, I realize that I am partly responsible for his death. But my responsibility is no greater than that of any member of the society that demanded this person's life. Certainly, it is no greater than that of the district attorney who prosecuted him, of the jury that brought in the verdict, of the judge who passed sentence, of the governor or pardon board that refused clemency, and of the warden and all the others upon whose shoulders rests the obligation of the state's legal killings.

As I have said before, the decision that a person must pay the supreme penalty has been reached long before the moment he is strapped in the electric chair, the head and leg electrodes and the mask are affixed, and I turn to the switch which will close the circuit. That decision was not mine. It was made by the state for which I am an instrument. Nothing that I could do would alter it.

Let us examine into the whole system that places an individual in the electric chair. The public needs protection against those who have no regard for decency I and law and order. To afford this, wrongdoers are punished. The people feel that in the case of murder and other serious crimes, the punishment should be severe—so severe, in fact, that it will serve as a deterrent. Consequently, through their duly elected representatives, they have declared these crimes to be capital offenses.

In a country like the United States, the law is what the majority of citizens want it to be. Otherwise, it is changed. The fact that capital punishment remains on the statute books of so many states, and that little or nothing is being done to erase it, is sufficient evidence that most of the people approve, or at least condone, this method of dealing with malefactors.

If a law is to be effective, it must, of course, be strictly enforced. Individuals must be chosen and empowered to carry out its provisions. There must be police, prosecutors, judges, juries, and prison wardens. There must be executioners, if the death penalty is to be exacted. Each and every one of these people is a part of society's plan to restrain and punish criminals. Each has an important role to play.

Remember that those who administer man's justice are not acting of their own accord. They are servants of the state, nothing more; and what they do is in compliance with the mandates of the public as expressed in the law. When they send a human being to his eternal doom, they do so only because it is their sworn duty.

That is my philosophy. It is not an attempt to justify my work. It is simply a statement of my honest belief.

Commenting on my line of reasoning, Elliott Roosevelt, son of the President, pointed out one night in a radio broadcast:

"He's right. We are the ones who say whether a man shall live or die. We could prescribe the alternative of life imprisonment if we desired."

On the subject of Ruth Snyder's execution, Mr. Roosevelt maintained:

"You and I sent Ruth Snyder to the electric chair. Oh yes, we did. But the public never likes to cut itself in on the blame. We like to watch those things from afar."

I know that there are many people who will not agree with this. Because mine is the one irrevocable act in a capital case, they will continue to regard me as a murderer. Moreover, they will never be willing to assume any responsibility for the taking of a human life.

Naturally, I have, at one time or another, thought of dying. I realize that it is certain and inescapable for all of us. But death and the world beyond hold no terrors for me. I see no reason why they should.

This will probably seem very strange to some people. They may wonder how a man who has snuffed out the lives of so many fellow beings could himself approach the end without fear in his heart. They doubtless think that he, of all people, should be afraid to breathe his last.

I will explain briefly why I am not. I have always been a God-fearing, religious person. I have endeavored to lead an honest, moral life, and in my dealings with others have tried to follow the Golden Rule. I have striven to be a good husband and a good father. Wherever I may have failed, it has not been for lack of sincere effort. As to the service I perform for the state, I have already discussed why in my mind there is no shadow of consciousness that I have done wrong.

It is generally assumed that, because of my occupation, I am in favor of capital punishment. Actually, I am not. I do not think that the death penalty is necessary to protect society, and do not believe that it should be inflicted. When I first entered the work, I had no particular views on the subject; but reached my conclusions after being official executioner for a number of years.

One of my predecessors, Edwin F. Davis, also saw no good reason why any person need die for the safety of the rest of us. On the day in 1903 when he electrocuted the three Van Wormer brothers, Davis told a newspaperman: "1 believe and hope that this execution will sound the beginning of the death knell of capital punishment in New York." I know he was sincere, for I often heard him express himself in a similar manner.

There are several reasons why the ancient law of "an eye for an eye and a tooth for a tooth" should be wiped from the statute books. First, man should not be permitted to destroy the one thing which cannot be restored—life. Furthermore, I believe that capital punishment serves no useful purpose, and is a form of revenge.

A wrong, no matter how serious, is not righted by ending a life. And if, as has happened, the condemned should not be guilty, then the tragedy is complete. These instances, of course, are very rare; but the judgment of juries is not infallible. There is always the possibility that an innocent person will pay the extreme penalty.

I thought of that not long ago while reading of a case in Michigan. A man was convicted of killing his neighbor, and was sent to prison for life—the maximum penalty for murder in that state. Nineteen years later, the case was reopened. Ballistic tests proved that the fatal bullet could not have been fired from his gun, so he was exonerated and set free. How fortunate it was that Michigan did not have capital punishment. Otherwise, a terrible mistake, which could not possibly have been rectified, would have been made.

Capital punishment, according to its advocates, is an effective deterrent of crime. But is it? Does the threat of the electric chair, the hangman's noose, the bullet, or lethal gas stay the hand of a potential murderer? I doubt it.

One night in 1930, I put two youths to death at Sing Sing for killing a man and his wife. The case had received quite some publicity, especially in and around New York City. On the day of the executions, drawings and photographs of the chair in which the pair were to die within a few hours were published in several newspapers. These should have been a warning to others, showing as they did the fate of convicted murderers in that state.

Yet, that very night, about the time the two youths walked their "last mile," a young hoodlum killed a New York policeman. Enraged because the officer had broken up a sidewalk dice game, he whipped out a gun and shot him. The fact that two others were forfeiting their lives for murder evidently had meant nothing to him.

On another night a few years later, I executed a man at Sing Sing for murdering a policeman. Before I reached home, two thugs in their early twenties slew an officer while they were robbing a New York establishment. The electrocution just an hour or so before had not restrained them.

All but six of our states impose the death penalty. Twenty-two states and the District of Columbia electrocute condemned prisoners, fourteen bring about legal death by hanging, five employ lethal gas, and one gives the prisoner a choice between hanging and shooting. But murder and other crimes punishable by death continue in these states; and in some, the murder rate has increased in recent years.

On the other hand, those states which have abolished capital punishment—Maine, Michigan, Minnesota, North Dakota, Rhode Island, and Wisconsin—have not been visited by any blight of murder. Their citizens have not found it necessary to take life in order to protect themselves.

Proponents of capital punishment argue that if the death penalty has failed in any respect as a crime de-

214

terrent, it is partly because too many of the condemned escape execution either through commutation of sentence or legal maneuvers. Although this may be true in a few states, it is not true for the country as a whole.

In the eight-year period from 1930 through 1937, state prisons received a total of 1,064 persons for execution. Of this number, 902—or nearly 85 per cent—were put to death. In other words, less than one-sixth of those sentenced to die were not executed. These statistics do not include the 413 persons who were executed in that period outside of prisons, such as in county jails in several of the Southern states.

One of the prices we pay for capital punishment is the opportunity it creates for a widespread orgy of sensationalism—almost sadism. Death is a fascinating subject to many people, perhaps because it marks the end of life and the beginning of the unknown. Consequently, the deliberate killing of a man or a woman by the state induces an excitement which in a notorious case becomes an emotional spree for those whose minds should not be so stimulated.

In my experience, I have seen a great deal of evidence of this. The crowds that waited outside the prisons for the executions of Sacco and Vanzetti, Ruth Snyder and Judd Gray, and Hauptmann are notable examples of what I mean. Many in those throngs were morbid individuals, to whom death is a commonplace jest and human life is cheap.

I recall a photograph published in a Boston newspaper on the day that the two Millen brothers and Abraham Faber died in Massachusetts' electric chair. The picture showed a crowd of curious people being held back by police outside the prison. In the front row, closest to the camera, were grinning boys and girls of twelve and fourteen. The death of three men inside the prison walls was their excuse for a lark that night.

But more shocking was an account I read of the Roman holiday provided by the hanging of a man at Owensboro, Kentucky, on August 14, 1936. No less than

215

twenty thousand–men, women, children, even babes in arms–watched the slayer-rapist plunge through the trap and dangle at the end of a rope. The huge crowd was in carnival-like spirits. People laughed, joked, shouted. They munched popcorn, sipped soft drinks, chewed at sandwiches. As soon as doctors pronounced the man dead, they tore off bits of the black hood for souvenirs. Then they merrily went their way. The primary purpose of the execution had been lost sight of by most of them. It had simply been a great show, something to talk about for a long time to come.

Unfortunately, with capital punishment comes vengeance. The two are inseparable. Revenge is present, if not predominant, in every case involving the death penalty. It is that, and little more, which is provided when I throw the switch to destroy a human life.

Certainly, it was the motivating impulse of the throng that jammed or stood outside the courthouse at Flemington, New Jersey, during the Hauptmann trial. These people and millions of others like them demanded– and finally got–satisfaction in death. The German carpenter had killed, they said, and the state, in turn, should do the same to him. No other punishment for his terrible crime would suffice.

That is also the way the family and friends of a little girl felt about the man who had criminally attacked and slain her. Death in the electric chair would be far too good for him, they declared. Something less humane should be his lot. When he escaped the supreme penalty by having his sentence commuted to life imprisonment, they were bitter. Justice had not been done, they cried.

There is another unfavorable aspect to capital punishment. Some jurors, even though theoretically approving the death penalty, are reluctant to assume the responsibility of deciding that a person shall lose his life. Consequently, first-degree murder convictions are often difficult to obtain, and criminals receive light sentences or are actually set free.

Of course, murder and other crimes of violence must be stamped out, and the penalty for such offenses must be severe. Death, however, is not the answer—no matter how humane the means. There is a less barbaric and a more just and intelligent way. The states in which capital punishment does not exist have found that way. They do not kill their criminals—they imprison them for life.

I believe that this should be the practice throughout the country. Furthermore, I believe that a sentence of life imprisonment should mean exactly that—a lifetime behind bars. There should be no lessening of the term and no pardon unless it is subsequently proved that justice has erred. Even then, this decision should rest with a court before which all the facts should be presented, and not with an individual or a small group.

Whether capital punishment will ever become only a grisly memory in the United States, no man knows. Today, according to surveys, the majority of the nation's voters favor the death penalty for murder. In my opinion, this sentiment will remain unchanged until the public is sufficiently aroused against the futility and needlessness of legally taking human life. Only by an intensive campaign of education will this be brought about.

So long as capital punishment exists, it would be wholly congruous to require any citizen to be present in the death chamber at the always awful moment when the spark of life is crushed from a man or a woman whom the state has doomed. That is, witnessing an execution would be made a civic duty, just as jury service has been. Thus would the repugnant horror of, and his responsibility in, legal slaying be impressed upon the average person. I venture to predict that if this were done, the abolishment of the death penalty would soon follow.

To me, the prevention of crime is vastly more important than punishment for it. Here society has failed in many respects. Before the problem can be approached intelligently, the basic causes of crime must be definitely established. These can be determined only by a careful study of innumerable criminal acts and the whole chain of events leading up to them. My records are most enlightening on this subject.

Of the nearly four hundred people I have put to death, one hundred and one murdered while committing a robbery; fifty-eight killed police officers; twenty slew in a fit of anger or while drunk; sixteen killed for profit, such as the collection of insurance money; twenty-seven committed sex murders, and six took life for revenge. The rest murdered under various other circumstances and for a number of reasons.

It is significant that the great majority of those who murdered while committing another crime were young men between the ages of eighteen and twenty-five. Most of them had not had the proper social, vocational, and religious training, so important to a youth in his formative years. Moreover, they had been reared under conditions of environment which were hardly conducive to a useful, honest life. In all too many instances, the parents were to blame.

One day a policeman whom I know told me of finding a twelve-year-old boy sleeping in an empty milk truck in a parking lot. He took the boy to the station house, fed him, and learned his name and address. The address was not more than a few blocks from where I live.

"Aren't your folks at home?" demanded the officer as he started out with the reluctant youngster, who did not want to go.

"I dunno. S'pose so," said the boy.

"How long is it since you've been home?" asked the policeman.

"Three days," was the reply. "How have you been eating?"

"Oh, by askin' people for somethin'," the young rascal said.

"Well, what's the idea of worrying your mother and father like this?" inquired the officer.

"Oh, I guess they don't worry so much," replied the youngster.

And the boy was right. At the house, the policeman woke up the family. He asked the mother why she had not reported her son's disappearance.

"He often goes away," she said, "but he always comes back."

"How do you think he's been eating?" the officer continued.

"I don't know," the mother answered. "He seems to get along somehow."

The policeman, himself a father, read that mother a midnight lesson on the responsibilities of parenthood. There are thousands of boys who leave home because of parental indifference, never to return. I am afraid I have met up with too many of them at the end of the trail—the electric chair in the prisons I serve.

Only a short time ago, I talked with a New York newspaperman, who is outstandingly successful in his field. He told me that one of the murderers whom I had executed at Sing Sing several years ago had been a member of his boyhood "gang" in Brooklyn.

"As boys in knee pants, we were all alike," he said. "We played pranks, hooked apples from fruit stands, outran the cops, and did the things that most city kids do. But Joe's parents drifted apart. No one kept after him to see that he stayed in school or that he held a job. He went from bad to worse. Finally, he decided that the world owed him a living, and one night found himself in a spot where he tried to shoot his way out. So you got him. I was luckier. I had somebody to keep an eye on me."

I think this is true enough. Yet, as the newspaperman spoke, my mind went back to the night of January 9, 1936, when four smooth-cheeked, intelligent-looking youths, two of them twenty-one, two of them only twenty, came to the chair at Sing Sing. It was the first time in several years that the bleak, bare walls of that brilliantly lighted chamber had seen as many as four men die within a few minutes. And never had four men so young died together. To me, there is, and always has been, something especially poignant in the execution of a young man to whom life's best things should still be beckoning.

The quartet–Newman Raymond, Jr., Amerigo Angelini, Thomas Gilbride, and Raymond K. Orley– were to forfeit their lives for the murder of a policeman. They had killed him when he surprised them in the act of robbing a New York luggage shop a year earlier.

Raymond was the son of a lay Methodist minister in a Southern town, and had had every advantage of a home in which good breeding, good books, and religious influences had pervaded the family circle. He was the first to go. As they lifted his limp body from the electric chair to the white wheel-table to trundle it into the autopsy room, his heartbroken mother was outside the prison gates in an automobile, where she had completely collapsed as the moment approached which she knew would end his life. The father had begged permission to accompany his son to the execution chamber, but his request had been denied. Here, certainly, was a case in which lack of training, guidance, and parental devotion could not be blamed for the fact that a young man had walked "the last mile."

Angelini was one who had had fewer advantages. But Gilbride had been a high school athlete, a boy who had enjoyed what we imagine is the valuable training afforded by athletic sports. Orley, also, was a product of circumstances which should have been conducive to a worth-while life.

Why, then, had they embarked on a career of crime?

To what could their untimely and ignominious end be attributed? The reason they were criminals was that they had come under the baleful influence of a man who, formerly a respected citizen, had shown them how to make "easy money." He had tutored them in the art of burglary, and they had been very successful until interrupted by the law.

The youths themselves answered the second question when they arrived at Sing Sing. Raymond said that the trouble he was in was due to "foolishness," and

Angelini gave the need of funds as the cause for his plight. Gilbride held evil associates responsible for the trail he blazed to the electric chair, and failure to attend church regularly was the reason advanced by Orley.

No matter why they were there, the state did not benefit one whit by putting them to death. These youths could have paid for their crimes with hard, useful labor within prison walls for the rest of their days. Society would have been safe, and justice would have been adequately served. But the state avenged a murder by writing an abrupt finis to four young lives; it made an "example" of them in the hope that potential malefactors would be restrained.

In spite of many executions every year, murder and other offenses punishable by death continue at an alarming rate. Of course, we will never know how many people may have been kept from the path of crime because of the fear of capital punishment. But as I study the records of those whom I have executed, and see how the threat of the death penalty failed to influence them, I cannot imagine that the number is large.

If I believed that capital punishment was an effective deterrent, and that society in general was safer and better off because of it, then I might be inclined to recognize a certain justification for the death penalty, regardless of my other objections. As it is, I hope that the day is not far distant when legal slaying, whether by electrocution, hanging, lethal gas, or any other method, is outlawed throughout the United States.

THE END

ABOUT THE AUTHOR

Robert Greene Elliott acted as state executioner for the States of New York, New Jersey, Vermont, Massachusetts, Pennsylvania and Connecticut during 1926 - 1939. He is often credited with perfecting the use of electrocution as a form of capital punishment and during his career he executed 387 condemned persons including some of the most famous criminal cases in the United States during the early 20th century.

Agent of Death, The Memoirs of an Executioner was originally published in 1940 and provides an intimate prospective into Robert Greene Elliott and his profession.

Made in the USA
Monee, IL
25 February 2024

54087805R00127